What They're Saying About B

"While there are excellent commentaries on the Bible, there are few books that are so rich in application-based understanding of the timeless truths of Proverbs as Bob Tamasy's *Business At Its Best*. These short chapters are perfect for small group studies, personal devotions and application, and insightful discussions of God's truths in Proverbs. I intend to personally use them in one of our local discussion groups." – *Don Mitchell, business consultant and former automobile manufacturing executive*

"*Business At Its Best* is a great business book – timely, insightful and down-to-earth. Bob Tamasy writes with style and elegant understanding of Proverbs and of life in business. This is must-reading for newcomers to the business world. But it is even more valuable for those of us who've already survived a few decades as corporate executives or entrepreneurs. Every businessman and woman in America should read and live by the wisdom of this important book." – *William L. Armstrong, former U.S. Senator, Colorado, entrepreneur and business executive*

"It's challenging in today's marketplace with the uncertainty of expanding globalization, outsourcing, and increased pressure to maintain profits – while facing ever increasing costs. How is a person to stay on track and maintain balance? Where is a business executive to turn? There are no simple solutions, but Robert Tamasy has written a great book that helps impart King Solomon's wisdom as revealed in the Book of Proverbs. In *Business At Its Best*, Bob writes in a clear and understandable way. He gets to the heart of the matter. He speaks clearly to the businessperson. I have recommended his book to friends and business colleagues. This book helps bring clear understanding for the busy and hassled businessperson. It is definitely a worthwhile read." – *Bob Milligan, Chairman, M. I. Industries, and Past President, CBMC International*

"How refreshing! *Business At Its Best* takes us back to the basics – to biblical wisdom from Proverbs that has stood the test of time. This is one of the most practical and helpful business books you'll ever read." – *John D. Beckett, Chairman, The Beckett Companies, and author,* Loving Monday: Succeeding in Business Without Selling Your Soul

BUSINESS AT ITS BEST

Expanded and Revised

BUSINESS AT ITS BEST

TIMELESS WISDOM FROM PROVERBS
FOR TODAY'S WORKPLACE

Robert J. Tamasy

Copyright © 2015 Robert J. Tamasy
All rights reserved.

ISBN: 151748362X
ISBN 13: 9781517483623
Library of Congress Control Number: 2015915785
CreateSpace Independent Publishing Platform
North Charleston, South Carolina

*This book is dedicated to the millions of men and women around the world
who faithfully strive to conduct their lives, businesses and careers
according to God's revealed truth in the Scriptures...*

*...And to those who have served as my teachers, examples and mentors
for more than three decades, demonstrating that the principles
in the Bible are not just for "the sweet by and by,"
but also for "the nasty now and now."*

TABLE OF CONTENTS

INTRODUCTION

BUSINESS AT ITS BEST

What is the best book on business that you have ever read? If you visit a typical bookstore, or browse the book section of an online retailer, you're likely to encounter hundreds of volumes on different aspects of business, many of them claiming to contain the ultimate secrets to success and professional achievement. Some are biographical, drawing insights from the lives of noted business leaders past and present. Others introduce multiple-step "how-to's" for becoming the next great executive or high-producing salesperson. Numerous books focus on motivation, trying to convince their readers that they can do whatever they set their minds to accomplish, while others convey important business truths through engaging little stories or allegories.

I've read and enjoyed dozens of these books. I won't list my "all-time best," but you might concur on some of my favorites. Through their pages I've encountered many worthwhile ideas and strategies. The breadth of thinking, range of experiences and variety of approaches is astounding. However, I don't think any collection of books in the business section could even approximate the depth and substance offered in what I consider the greatest business book ever written – the Bible. In fact, we can discover more practical business wisdom presented in just one small section of the Bible, the 31-chapter book of Proverbs, than we would find in any other book, even those written by today's foremost authorities on the global marketplace.

This, of course, is my opinion. I invite you to take an honest look at the "evidence" yourself and then arrive at your own verdict. I would be interested in knowing what you think. Over the concise chapters that follow, you will have the opportunity to consider many of the practical, amazingly contemporary truths the ancient book of Proverbs teaches on such varied topics as integrity, honesty, communications, interpersonal relationships, anger, greed, handling money, hard work, competition, and others. In fact, even though it was written and compiled thousands of years ago, Proverbs presents workplace guidelines, challenges and warnings that could just as easily have been penned in the 21st century.

When this book was originally published in 2005, it consisted of 40 chapters. I've expanded it to a total of 53, one for every week of the year – and one for good measure. I've entitled this new section, "Perspectives Beyond Proverbs." So if you'd like to read and reflect on a single chapter a week that would be fine with me. The additional chapters draw primarily from other passages in the Bible, showing the useful business wisdom of the Scriptures isn't restricted to Proverbs.

King Solomon of Israel was the primary writer of Proverbs, and in another of his books in the Bible he wrote, "there is nothing new under the sun" (Ecclesiastes 1:9). Perhaps this is one reason that despite the passage of many centuries, the wisdom of Proverbs remains so fresh and relevant now. Many "revolutionary" business concepts being published today are nothing more than old ideas that have been tried and proved true over and over – and have never failed. Eternal truths have no expiration date.

One of the most intriguing realities is that the principles from Proverbs apply to the world of business and work even for those who are not religious, or even spiritual. These timeless principles work for one reason: because they're true. They are not absolute promises in all cases, but they definitely are probabilities that have proved valid countless times. Truth has a way of holding its own, regardless of ideologies, predispositions or agendas.

But before we look at how Proverbs treats dozens of topics pertinent to today's business world, let me ask a question: What's the difference between *knowledge* and *wisdom*? A business consultant friend of mine explains it this way: Knowledge involves simply knowing, "what is." Wisdom involves knowing, "what is right."

In business, it's not unusual to take shortcuts. We employ them in trying to close an important sale or achieve a desired profit in the shortest possible length of time, even if this involves wandering into the gray areas of right and wrong. Success in the short-term, however, does not always translate into success in the long-term. That's why *wisdom,* and not *knowledge,* should be especially prized in the business and professional world.

But how do we acquire this necessary wisdom? Proverbs is among the books of the Bible classified as "wisdom literature," and appropriately, Proverbs' opening chapters offer insights about the how's, why's and where's of wisdom:

We can learn and seek guidance from others. *"Let the wise listen and add to their learning, and let the discerning get guidance"* (Proverbs 1:5).

Wisdom can keep us out of harm's way. *"For the waywardness of the simple will kill them, and the complacency of fools will destroy them; but whoever listens to me (wisdom) will live in safety and be at ease, without fear of harm"* (Proverbs 1:32-33).

Ultimately, wisdom is a gift from God. *"...then you will understand the fear of the Lord and find the knowledge of God. For the Lord gives wisdom, and from his mouth come knowledge and understanding"* (Proverbs 2:5-6).

Wisdom offers protection from unscrupulous, destructive influences. *"Discretion will protect you, and understanding will guard you. Wisdom will save you from the ways of wicked men, from men whose words are perverse"* (Proverbs 2:11-12).

Eugene Peterson, compiler of a popular, best-selling paraphrase of the Bible called *The Message,* makes this observation: "Many people think that what's written in the Bible has mostly to do with getting people into heaven – getting right with God, saving their eternal souls. It does have to do with that, of course, but not *mostly.* It is equally concerned with living on this earth – living well, living in robust sanity. In our Scriptures, heaven is not the primary concern, to which earth is a tag-a-long after-thought. 'On earth *as* it is in heaven' is Jesus' prayer."

Tagging along with Peterson's last comment, it's reasonable to assume that as Jesus prayed and spoke of "on earth," He might well have been including the corporate boardroom, the office cubicle, the receptionist desk, the sales territory, the airport, and even the home office.

So let's get started in learning what this sampling of the wisdom from Proverbs has to say specifically and practically to those of us who labor, in one way or another, in the ever-changing, stress-filled business and professional world of the 21st century.

Occasionally in the Proverbs chapters, when appropriate, I've invoked my literary license to include portions of other Scriptures. Most of the last 13 chapters, as I've noted, draw deeply from other passages in the Bible, showing the harmony and consistency of biblical truth from front to back.

I hope you encounter more than one "aha" experience during the course of reading this book. It may even prompt you to conduct further investigation on your own. I also hope you will find the application questions at the end of each chapter, "Putting It into Practice," useful for personal reflection and/or group discussion.

Robert J. Tamasy
Chattanooga, TN
2015

CHAPTER 1

STICKING WITH THE TRIED, TESTED AND TRUE

D o you ever become distressed with things don't work as they should – or at least the way you *think* they should? Maybe it's when your computer freezes up without warning, and you're in the midst of an urgent, time-sensitive project. Or when your car won't start and you're already late for an appointment. Or you're stuck at a location where you discover you can't get a signal for your cell phone, making it impossible to make that important call.

Recently I found myself perturbed when the ATM machine I usually use near my home was not in operation. I put my ATM card in the slot, and the computerized message board informed me, "Sorry. Machine is temporarily out of service." Terrific! That was the third time the machine had malfunctioned for me in less than a month, and I was aggravated. "Now what am I going to do?" I asked myself. I needed some cash, but didn't want to drive several miles to my bank's next closest ATM machine. And I hate having to pay a fee for using another bank's ATM.

Suddenly a memory from the distant past surfaced. "What did I do before ATM machines were invented?" I wondered. Then I remembered: "I would just write a check to myself and cash it!" As it happened, I had my checkbook with me, so I parked my car, went into the bank and wrote a check for the amount I needed. This solution was simple enough, but had almost become obscured by the complexities of modern electronic technology.

If you're old enough to sometimes wonder how you survived without a word processor, cell phone, e-mail, fax machines, the Internet, texting, overnight mail and other innovations of the past several decades, you're not alone. It's amazing how quickly we become accustomed to the latest advancements, to the point where we forget how to function without them. For instance, being a professional writer, I would never give up my computer and return to an electric typewriter. It would seem like traveling back into prehistoric times and carving words in stone. The so-called "good old days," in reality, weren't all that good in many cases!

But some things in life, unlike technological wonders, are not subject to relentless change and improvement. Consider wisdom for one. There are many factors that contribute to success in the workplace, but wisdom would have to rank at or near the top. Impressive degrees from prestigious universities and colleges may affirm that you have obtained knowledge, perhaps even the best knowledge that money can buy, but that doesn't mean you've gained wisdom – or have any idea about how to use it if you had it.

I remember a friend at work who had never spent a day in college. He didn't hold a prominent position in our company, but when I needed down-to-earth, practical wisdom to assist in making a critical decision, I often would consult him. His common sense responses taught me several things about the importance of wisdom – in business and in life. Consider what the book of Proverbs tells us about wisdom:

Wisdom is invaluable. *"Blessed is the man who finds wisdom, the man who gains understanding, for she is more profitable than silver and yields better returns than gold"* (Proverbs 3:13-14).

Wisdom does not have to be heard. *"Wise men store up knowledge, but the mouth of a fool invites ruin"* (Proverbs 10:14).

Wisdom is admired. *"A man is praised according to his wisdom, but men with warped minds are despised"* (Proverbs 12:8).

Wisdom weighs the consequences. *"The wisdom of the prudent is to give thought to their ways, but the folly of fools is deception"* (Proverbs 14:8).

Wisdom gives direction, charting a safe course. *"Folly delights a man who lacks judgment, but a man of understanding keeps a straight course"* (Proverbs 15:21).

Wisdom helps to maintain focus. *"A discerning man keeps wisdom in view, but a fool's eyes wander to the ends of the earth"* (Proverbs 17:24).

PUTTING IT INTO PRACTICE

1. On a scale of 1 to 10, 1 being the lowest and 10 being the highest, how would you rate yourself when it comes to wisdom?

2. How do you react to the thought that wisdom is a key factor in achieving success in the business world?

3. Who are some of the wisest people you know? Why do you consider them to be wise?

4. What steps do you think could be helpful in enhancing the wisdom that you possess, both personally and professionally?

CHAPTER 2

WHERE DO YOU GO FOR GUIDANCE?

Our world has become increasingly complex, in virtually every conceivable way – technologically, economically, sociologically, politically, vocationally, and so on. So when the time comes to make important decisions, the stakes are higher and factors to be considered are more complicated.

Seemingly simple decisions like starting up a website, developing a corporate mission statement, or even determining which financial institution to do business with, can prove to be very stressful. I have lived long enough to realize I don't have all the answers. In fact, sometimes I'm not even sure what the right questions are! For that reason, when I face a crucial decision – whether it involves a possible career change, buying a car, or how to address a difficult situation in my family – I often turn to trusted friends for advice. Over and over I have found truth in the statement, "Not one of us (alone) is as smart as all of us (together)."

BETTER TWO THAN ONE

If you read the book of Proverbs, you'll find it repeatedly encourages us to seek counsel – and to be open to those who volunteer helpful advice. For instance, it underscores the value of working with others: *"As iron sharpens iron, so one man sharpens another"* (Proverbs 27:17). This principle is stated differently in another part of the Bible: *"Two are better than one, because they have a good return for their work.... A cord of three strands is not quickly broken"* (Ecclesiastes 4:9-12).

Sometimes we receive counsel when we're not really asking for it (or prepared to receive it), but if we're wise we will listen anyway and consider it carefully. If the advice comes from someone who really cares about us and is looking out for our best interests, it could be a precious gift. *"Perfume and incense bring joy to the heart, and the pleasantness of one's friend springs from his earnest counsel"* (Proverbs 27:9).

Here are some other principles from Proverbs about the seeking – and receiving – of advice and counsel:

Before taking any major action, seek guidance. Too often, we act first and then wonder about possible consequences. A person of wisdom avoids acting hastily. Wise counselors can point out flaws in our thinking in advance, helping us to avoid disaster. *"Make plans by seeking advice; if you wage war, obtain guidance"* (Proverbs 20:18). *"A wise man has great power, and a man of knowledge increases strength; for waging war you need guidance, and for victory many advisers"* (Proverbs 24:5-6).

Wise counsel helps to bring about the desired result. Sometimes we become so determined to follow a course of action, we forget – or choose not – to consult with others in advance. In reality, they might support our decision, but at the same time could help to identify some weaknesses in our plan that we're unable or unwilling to see. As the adage says, "Sometimes you can't see the forest for the trees." Trusted counselors can assist us in achieving our objectives with a minimum of pain or difficulty. *"For lack of guidance a nation falls, but many advisers make victory sure"* (Proverbs 11:14). *"Plans fail for lack of counsel, but with many advisers they succeed"* (Proverbs 15:22).

Choose your advisers carefully. When seeking counsel and direction in making important decisions, be cautious not to seek out only people that will tell you what you want to hear. Go to people who have genuine interest in you and have special experience and insight about the issues you are facing. Then consider what they tell you very seriously. *"The plans of the righteous are just, but the advice of the wicked is deceitful"* (Proverbs 12:5).

Just because a decision seems right or feels right, that doesn't mean it actually *is* right. Sometimes emotion or personal biases can cloud our judgment; we may want something so much that we're determined to pursue it no matter what. Someone has said that when it comes to important decisions, we tend to base our decisions on emotion and then attempt to justify those decisions with selectively chosen facts. At such times, when the risk of becoming blinded by subjectivity is so great, wise and objective advice is needed more than ever. *"The way of a fool seems right to him, but a wise man listens to advice"* (Proverbs 12:15).

Putting It into Practice

1. What is your typical style in making decisions: Do you arrive at your conclusions quickly, or do you approach the issue methodically and carefully, weighing all the relevant factors before formulating a final conclusion?

2. Do you agree that the complexities of life, particularly in today's workplace, have made the decision-making process more difficult? Why or why not?

3. Do you have any trusted friends or peers to whom you can turn for wise counsel when needed? If so, what makes you believe their advice and insights are reliable?

4. Have you ever followed someone's counsel or advice, only to learn too late that they were wrong? What was the situation – and what would you do differently if a similar situation were to present itself to you today?

CHAPTER 3

FINDING HOPE IN HARD WORK

Years ago, I had a friend who would often say, "I love hard work. I can sit for hours at a time and watch people that are doing it." You may know some people like that. They don't mind hard work, as long as it's someone else expending the sweat and energy. Apparently the "work-inhibited" expect that the resources for what they need each day – and for what they desire – will somehow come their way with little or no effort. But then, if they should see others prospering and advancing personally and professionally, while they aren't, these same people would feel resentful and cry, "Unfair!"

I know of two men who as teenagers were both accomplished athletes. Both had the raw potential to succeed at the professional sports level. One man applied himself, diligently refining his strengths and skills, while working hard to overcome his weaknesses. Eventually he progressed to the top professional level of his sport and became a "star" for more than a decade.

The other man, who was the same age and had grown up in the same city, expected opportunities to simply be handed to him, with little effort on his part. When he made mistakes, he preferred to offer excuses rather than to acknowledge his failings or work fervently to eliminate or reduce deficiencies in his athletic prowess. Instead of becoming a star, he chose to become a sluggard – someone whose laziness and lack of initiative turns "what could have been" into "never will be." The closest this second man has ever come to professional sports is buying a ticket to attend a game as a spectator.

Most of us have never been accused of being world-class athletes, but we all have unique strengths and skills that, if refined and cultivated, could chart a course to success. But it requires work – hard work. The alternative is to relegate ourselves to the role of spectators, similar to the friend I mentioned earlier whose enjoyment of work is confined to observing it being performed by others. People like this may never achieve the success they desire, but at least they won't have to break a sweat.

In regard to the realm of hard work and diligence, the ancient book of Proverbs offers an assortment of principles that remain amazingly relevant and practical for the 21st century workplace. Here are some of them:

Hard work is motivated by need. If we had someone who guaranteed to pay for all of our expenses, or if we suddenly became wealthy beyond imagination, we probably would lose motivation for working as hard as we should. But when we have a need to fulfill, we suddenly realize how important it is to apply ourselves diligently to our work responsibilities. *"The laborer's appetite works for him; his hunger drives him on"* (Proverbs 16:26).

Hard work often results in honor. Because relatively few people truly make the commitment to work hard, pouring everything they have into the task at hand and utilizing their abilities to the maximum, they tend to be noticed. Often these are the individuals who receive promotions and special recognition for contributions to their companies. *"Do you see a man skilled in his work? He will serve before kings; he will not serve before obscure men"* (Proverbs 22:29). *"He who tends a fig tree will eat its fruit, and he who looks after his master will be honored"* (Proverbs 27:18).

Hard work prepares for leadership responsibilities. Who would you rather work for – someone that sets the example through his or her own diligent efforts, or someone who sits back preferring to let everyone else do the work? When you consistently set the pace in working hard, it is likely that one day you will be asked to show others how to do the same. *"Diligent hands will rule, but laziness ends in slave labor"* (Proverbs 12:24).

Hard work yields lasting results. Sometimes we're tempted to act in haste, wanting to "work a deal" that promises to bring a rapid and substantial financial return. However, acting hastily can bring devastating results if we have failed to anticipate potential problems. Working diligently may take longer, and the immediate financial return typically is not nearly as great, but in the long term it proves to be the wisest course. *"The plans of the diligent lead to profit as surely as haste leads to poverty* (Proverbs 21:5).

Putting It into Practice

1. Reread some of the verses included in this chapter – Proverbs 16:26, Proverbs 21:5, Proverbs 22:29, and Proverbs 27:18. Which of them seem to have particular significance to you?

2. How do you respond to the following statements?

   a. Hard work is motivated by need.

   b. Hard work often results in honor.

   c. Hard work prepares for leadership responsibilities.

   d. Hard work yields lasting results.

3. Do you think that hard work ensures success? Why or why not?

4. Even if you can't receive a 100 percent guarantee of being able to succeed according to your expectations, should you still strive to work as hard as possible and remain dedicated to excellence regardless of the results? Explain your answer.

CHAPTER 4

ANGER: A DANGEROUS AND UNNECESSARY TOOL

Years ago I was working on the news desk of a suburban daily newspaper, being groomed to replace the news editor who was leaving to do post-graduate work at a prestigious university. Since he was the veteran newsman, possessing years of experience, I as the relative novice was eager to observe what he did and how he did it so I could follow his example when I succeeded him.

The news editor, however, had an unpredictable and sometimes explosive temper. I remember one morning he was reviewing an article prior to publication –it might even have been one that I had been working on. For some reason, this editor suddenly became enraged and randomly threw a wooden ruler he was holding. This ruler had a metal straight-edge and, when tossed with force, could easily have turned into a dangerous weapon. Fortunately, by mere inches, the measuring instrument whizzed past the ear of one of our reporters. Had ruler and reporter's head made contact, the injury probably would have been considerable, but in his anger the editor seemed oblivious to the potential damage his outburst had nearly inflicted.

As it happened, at the time I was battling periodic episodes of anger myself. I recognized the risk of hurling lethal objects, but my honest impression at the time was that a display of anger was one way to demonstrate my commitment and determination to doing a job properly. Since then, however, my perspectives on anger – and its role in the workplace – have changed.

Many times anger is used to coerce people into doing what we want them to do. Anger can cause fear, and fearful people often become more compliant. Anger also results from pent-up frustrations that arise from unmet expectations, the failure of well-conceived plans, and the disconcerting tendency for things to go wrong at the most inopportune moments, along with many other causes. Feeling angry may be a very understandable and natural emotion, but one characteristic of a truly excellent business or professional person is how anger is expressed.

The book of Proverbs offers an abundance of wise insight and counsel about anger and its potential dangers. So much, in fact, that we will look at some of the principles below, and then offer another appraisal of anger in a later chapter. Here are some realities about the effects of anger in the workplace:

Show self-control. Instead of showing anger when someone offends you, demonstrate your personal control and character by not responding in a similar manner. *"A fool shows his annoyance at once, but a prudent man overlooks an insult"* (Proverbs 12:16).

Controlled anger shows wisdom. Anger can cause people to react impulsively, preventing them from properly evaluating circumstances that have made them angry. *"A patient man has great understanding, but a quick-tempered man displays folly"* (Proverbs 14:29). *"A fool gives full vent to his anger, but a wise man keeps himself under control"* (Proverbs 29:11).

Remaining calm can keep a conflict from intensifying. Have you ever noticed that when someone is speaking loudly, even shouting, if another person chooses to respond quietly and calmly, the tension in the situation quickly begins to dissipate? *"A hot-tempered person stirs up dissension, but a patient man calms a quarrel"* (Proverbs 15:18).

Anger can prompt words that are regretted later. When angry, it's easy to express hurtful thoughts you may be feeling at the moment, only to wish later that you could retract those harsh words. *"A man of knowledge uses words with restraint, and a man of understanding is even-tempered"* (Proverbs 17:27).

Trying to protect an angry person can be futile. Sometimes we appoint ourselves peacemakers, attempting to intervene for a person whose anger has gone out of control. This may help, but it also might merely postpone inevitable consequences for someone given to habitually venting emotions without restraint. *"A hot-tempered man must pay the penalty; if you rescue him, you will have to do it again"* (Proverbs 19:19)

Don't emulate the behavior of angry people. While working with the temperamental editor, I began to imitate his actions, thinking this was suitable, even desirable behavior under the pressure of imminent deadlines. However, displaying similar outbursts did nothing to enhance either my performance or my reputation. *"Do not make friends with a hot-tempered man, do not associate with one easily angered, or you may learn his ways and get yourself ensnared"* (Proverbs 22:24-25).

Putting It into Practice

1. Think of a specific time when you have seen anger being displayed in the workplace. Was it demonstrated in an appropriate or inappropriate way? Explain.

2. In general, do you think improper displays of anger are a common problem in the business world today? Why do you think that is the case – or isn't?

3. Is anger an emotion you struggle with personally? If you do, can you think of a situation that is fairly typical for you? How might the wisdom in the passages cited from Proverbs help with keeping anger in check?

4. When someone gets angry with you, how do you typically respond? What might be some possible solutions for the "chronically angry" – and for the "victims" who have to deal with them?

CHAPTER 5

DILIGENCE PAVES THE WAY TO PROSPERITY

Wouldn't it be nice to become instantly wealthy, to wake up one morning knowing you'll no longer have any financial worries? Can you imagine the freedom that could bring to your life?

The idea of "getting rich quick" appeals to many of us. In the U.S.A., a number of states sponsor lotteries that award millions of dollars to the winners. Many people engage in various forms of gambling, games of chance in which they hope the money they put at risk will become multiplied if they win. (That "IF" may be the largest two-letter word in the world.)

The Internet and ordinary email are not immune to this yearning to become rich without doing much – if anything – to gain the wealth. Websites offer contests that anyone can enter, promising thousands for the winners. And recently I have received emails promising two ways to becoming instantly wealthy. One was a "chain letter," advising the reader to send a small sum of money to the top several individuals on a list, assuring that within weeks those who send the money will themselves begin to reap hundreds and even thousands of dollars. Another email promised I could share in a huge fortune if I would help in recovering funds that had been deposited in a bank in a distant land. All I needed to do was to invest a sizable sum myself to get the process started.

Yes, instant wealth sounds enticing. But experience teaches that the best way to become prosperous is through a strategy that has been utilized for countless centuries. You know what this strategy is? I'm going to tell you; let you in on the secret. Get out a pen and notebook so you can write it down and have it readily accessible whenever you need a reminder.

This strategy is: *Diligence and hard work.*

Wait! Weren't we talking about getting rich *instantly?* Hard work takes a long time, right? Yes, but there is an old saying: "Easy come, easy go." If money comes without effort, it can depart just as easily. Proverbs has much to say about diligence and hard work. Let's look at just a sampling of the principles it offers:

Work looking to the future. Too often we consider only the present, presuming future necessities will somehow take care of themselves. But we have a familiar example from nature that shows such thinking is foolish. *"Go to the ant, you sluggard; consider its ways and be wise! It has no commander, no overseer or ruler, yet it stores its provisions in summer and gathers its food at harvest"* (Proverbs 6:6-8).

Laziness leads to poverty. Money does not grow on trees, or materialize magically out of nowhere. It is the byproduct of hard work. *"How long will you lie there, you sluggard? When will you get up from your sleep? A little sleep, a little slumber, a little folding of the hands to rest – and poverty will come on you like a bandit and scarcity like an armed man"* (Proverbs 6:9-11).

Diligence leads to wealth. If we use our skills, talents and experience diligently and faithfully, our work eventually will be rewarded. *"Lazy hands make a man poor, but diligent hands bring wealth"* (Proverbs 10:4).

Talk is cheap; work pays the bills. Have you ever been around someone who talks incessantly about what he plans to do, but never does anything? These are the same people who complain about never having what they need, of never getting the "breaks" to realize their dreams. *"All hard work brings a profit, but mere talk leads only to poverty"* (Proverbs 14:23).

You reap what you sow. If you make the right preparations, and invest enough time and energy at the beginning, you most likely will realize a pleasing and satisfactory return at the end. *"A sluggard does not plow in season; so at harvest time he looks but finds nothing"* (Proverbs 20:4).

PUTTING IT INTO PRACTICE

1. Do you find yourself spending much time thinking about, even strategizing about, what you could do if you were to receive a financial windfall?

2. Imagine that you one day were to receive such a monetary boon. How do you think you would use it?

3. How would you rate yourself as a worker, in terms of the typical effort and determination you expend in pursuing your assignments and responsibilities?

4. Can you think of a time when you had no choice but to persevere and work diligently to achieve a personal, professional or financial goal? How did it feel when you finally reached your objective?

5. Do you believe the adage, "you reap what you sow"? Why or why not?

It is even said that we reap far more than what we sow, using the example of planting a grain of corn and harvesting an entire stalk. Can you think of any examples of this truism in your life?

CHAPTER 6

CAN YOU COMPETE – WITHOUT COMPARING?

Competition, whether it takes place in an athletic arena or a place of business, can be a good thing. It can motivate us to work harder, refine our skills, and reach deeply within ourselves to perform as well as we possibly can.

Even if we're engaged in a friendly game of golf, racquetball or tennis, playing someone better than ourselves can raise our own level of play. On a sports team, the challenge of competing for a starting position can result in everyone showing significant improvement. And competition in the workplace – whether within our companies or with rival businesses – can prove beneficial for everyone involved. Customers and clients benefit because they can be assured of receiving our very best in our desire to attract or retain their business. Workers, spurred on by congenial competition with their associates, experience the joy of knowing they have given their maximum effort. And employers reap the financial harvest of productive employees working with enthusiasm.

However, danger also lurks in the shadows of competition. This danger becomes reality when competition yields to comparison, often disintegrating into envy and jealousy.

We probably all can think of times when healthy competition gradually deteriorated into unhealthy comparison. Such as when a much-desired and well-deserved promotion went to someone else. Or when a coworker received a substantial pay raise or bonus and we didn't. Fear of falling short when being compared with others can tempt us to make un-ethical compromises; "the end justifies the means" becomes the defense, even though it's a very weak rationalization.

So how do we enjoy the benefits of competition, while avoiding the potential pitfalls of comparison? Once again, we find great wisdom from Proverbs:

Always strive to be at peace. When we compete fairly and equitably, we can be at peace with ourselves – and with our peers. Our victories need not come at the expense of others. But when we compete to win "at any cost," unhealthy conflict becomes inevitable. If how we're comparing with others stands paramount in our minds, competition becomes dis-eased. *"A heart at peace gives life to the body, but envy rots the bones"* (Proverbs 14:30).

To maintain strong relationships, sometimes less is more. Harmony and cooperation in the workplace – as well as in the home and with friends – are prized commodities, but they can't exist in an environment of bitter competition and comparison. If we value our relationships, sometimes it might be worth settling for a bit less than we would prefer. *"Better a meal of vegetables where there is love than a fattened calf with hatred"* (Proverbs 15:17).

The cost of comparison is conflict. There is something very appealing about being able to go to work without the dread of dealing with hostil-ity, and being able to go to sleep unhindered by unnecessary anxieties and anger. One way to achieve this is by competing fairly and without un-necessary comparison. *"Better a dry crust with peace and quiet than a house full of feasting, with strife"* (Proverbs 17:1).

Jealousy from comparison results in devastation. In chapter 4 we looked at the harmful effects of uncontrolled anger. Jealousy can have an even more destructive impact. There may be times when we feel unfairly treat-ed, or that others have received inequitable advantages. Our perceptions may be true, but festering jealousy can act like an uncontrolled cancer. Eventually it kills – relationships, hopes, reputations, even careers. *"Anger is cruel and fury overwhelming, but who can stand before jealousy?"* (Proverbs 27:4).

PUTTING IT INTO PRACTICE

1. Not everyone has the same competitive drive. How competitive do you regard yourself? Is it always important for you to "win" – at work, as well as at play?

2. Have you observed the detrimental effects of mixing competition with comparison? Be honest: How well are you able to compete – in the workplace or in leisure activities – without measuring or comparing yourself or your performance with others?

3. Do you believe that all-out competition – even if it costs relationships or peace of mind – is merited? Is that just "reality" in today's business and professional world? Explain your answer.

4. Are there any current situations in which you feel envy or jealousy toward others? Whether you're experiencing those emotions at present, or have felt them in the past, have they ever succeeded in bringing about a positive outcome? Elaborate on your answer.

CHAPTER 7

HOW MUCH IS A REPUTATION WORTH?

Who would you rather do business with – a person with a strong, commendable reputation, or with someone of questionable, even dubious character? You might be thinking, "That's a silly question. Of course I would want to conduct business with someone who has a good reputation!"

Let me ask a similar question, but one that is perhaps a bit harder to answer: Would you rather have a good reputation and have to face financial challenges each month – or be wealthy, but with a bad reputation?

The truth is, a good reputation does not necessarily guarantee financial and business success, and some people manage to prosper in spite of having an unsavory reputation in the business and professional world. However, the person with the good reputation – one who is known for qualities such as integrity, fairness, diligence and excellence – might find it easier to sleep well at night, untroubled by a guilty conscience or fear of repercussions from unscrupulous behavior.

It has been observed that a good reputation can only be built over a lifetime, but can be destroyed beyond repair in a relatively short span of time, even a single moment. It may seem unfair that an isolated indiscretion, or one questionable business deal, could undermine an otherwise flawless personal and professional record, but it's a fact just the same. Trust and confidence are gained – and sustained – one day at a time, minute by minute. Each day presents a new opportunity to prove we are who we claim to be. But once trust is shattered, whether in business or a relationship, it can be regained only with great difficulty, if at all.

Have you ever had someone make a promise to you – a firm commitment – only to have them fail in fulfilling that promise? How did you feel at the time? How easy was it for you to trust that person the next time he or she "promised" or vowed to do something that was important to you?

I don't know about you, but I can think of several times when I failed to keep personal commitments. To this day, I regret these failures. In the process of maturing, I've come to realize the importance and immense value of a sterling reputation, of being a person who does what he says he will do. This is one reason the Bible urges, *"Let your 'Yes' be yes, and your 'No,' no..."* (James 5:12). This is also one reason the ancient book of Proverbs has assigned such high value to having and maintaining a good reputation. Let's consider a few of its observations on the topic:

The sterling reputation. Wealth can be acquired in many ways, and precious metals and gems can be purchased, but even the most exclusive retail store cannot sell you a good reputation. It's not a commodity to be purchased or bartered; it can only be obtained through a life devoted to upholding high ideals and personal values – even when it's not convenient or expedient. *"A good name is more desirable than great riches; to be esteemed is better than silver or gold"* (Proverbs 22:1).

The squandered reputation. Being "trustworthy" literally means being worthy of someone's trust at all times, not just at those times when it's convenient and in our best interests. Like it or not, the moment we betray a trust is the moment we suddenly become unworthy of being trusted in the future. *"If you argue your case with a neighbor, do not betray another man's confidence, or he who hears it may shame you and you will never lose your bad reputation"* (Proverbs 25:9-10).

The shining reputation. Living in a world filled with broken promises, where so many people seem dedicated solely to furthering their own self-interests, the person with an established, good reputation is becoming something of a curiosity, a rarity. At the same time, this person is someone that others readily seek out, a bit like being drawn to a single, small light in a darkened room. *"The path of the righteous is like the first gleam of dawn, shining ever brighter till the full light of day. But the way of the wicked is like deep darkness; they do not know what makes them stumble"* (Proverbs 4:18-19).

Putting It into Practice

1. Who comes to your mind when you think of someone with a good reputation? Conversely, can you think of anyone you know or work with who serves as an example of someone with a bad or questionable reputation? How would you compare them? What is the difference?

2. How would you assess your own reputation – among your peers, among your customers or clients in business, even within your own family?

3. Why do you think it is so difficult to gain and maintain a good reputation, but so easy to lose it?

4. What steps do you think you can take – or should take – to ensure that your reputation remains strong and positive? Would it help if you had the support, even the accountability, of some other individuals? Explain.

CHAPTER 8

A FEW WELL-CHOSEN WORDS CAN GO A LONG WAY

We seem to be immersed in the age of the talk show, both on TV and radio. Men and women have become highly paid celebrities on TV simply because of their skills at speaking – and interviewing other people. Many hosts of radio talk shows may never become famous or wealthy, but that doesn't hinder them from talking and expressing their ideas on a seemingly limitless variety of topics. It seems the motto for some talk show personalities is, "I have and will express an opinion on everything – whether I know anything about it or not!"

In the business and professional world, individuals who like to talk often seem to be rewarded for their multitude of words. We see sales and marketing people working hard to persuade others with their clever words and lines of reasoning. Business meetings are often dominated by a few people with powerful personalities and a penchant for pushing their points of view.

What about people who are shy, not as eloquent, or as quick with the tongue – is there any hope for them? Actually, those who choose to speak more sparingly often earn admiration and respect for their careful and judicious use of language.

I know a highly regarded member of a corporate board who was widely admired because he refused to speak with reckless abandon. While others were talking at great length, he would restrict himself to actively and intently listening and thinking. And when he spoke, what this leader had to say was always worth considering. Years ago an investment company used the slogan, "When E. F. Hutton speaks, people listen." This man could have been described in the same way.

Over the years I have increasingly made it my goal to apply the time-tested advice to *"...be quick to listen, slow to speak..."* (James 1:19). I would like to think I'm making some progress in this area, although that is not my natural tendency. Too often I've been slow to listen (and think), and quick to speak. To put it in automotive vernacular, I have had a strong inclination to put my mouth in drive while my brain is still in park!

Let's take a look at some of the other excellent insights that Proverbs offers regarding the power – and perils – of the tongue:

Many words can lead to inappropriate, even harmful comments. Have you ever been involved in a discussion that was going well until you said something spontaneously – and then wished you could retract those words? The fact is, the fewer words you speak, the less chance you will have of saying something you will later regret. *"When words are many, sin is not absent, but he who holds his tongue is wise"* (Proverbs 10:19).

Many words do not necessarily demonstrate knowledge. We may feel the need to impress people by how much we have to say about a topic. Often, however, a speaker can accomplish more with a minimum of well-chosen, carefully considered words expressed in just a few moments than by engaging in a diatribe that seems to continue without end. *"A man of knowledge uses words with restraint, and a man of understanding is even-tempered"* (Proverbs 17:27).

Many words often cause trouble. Have you ever known anyone who seemed determined to voice feelings and opinions, regardless of whether they were invited or welcomed to do so? I describe such people as those who delight in giving someone a piece of their mind that they cannot afford to lose! The adage, "Sticks and stones may break my bones, but names will never hurt me" is a lie – because harmful words many times remain with us long after physical wounds have healed. Foolish, unthinking statements can offend unnecessarily, and they can ruin long-cherished friendships. Even if what we say is true, we would be well-advised to contemplate how we express it – and when. Before speaking the truth, consider the consequences. *"He who guards his mouth and tongue keeps himself from calamity"* (Proverbs 21:23).

Putting It into Practice

1. Are you a person who is quick and eager to express your feelings and opinions? Why or why not?

2. Can you think of times when problems resulted after you – or someone you know – made statements that would have been better left unsaid? Give an example and think about or discuss what resulted.

3. What steps would you suggest for someone who needs to learn how to be "quick to listen and slow to speak"?

4. Being truthful is a virtue, but do you think there times when telling the truth can be harmful? Does not telling the truth always amount to lying to someone? Explain your answer.

5. What guidelines can we use for determining when, and how, to communicate the truth to others when they may not want to hear it, much less start to act upon what we have to say?

CHAPTER 9

THE BURDENSOME BUSINESS OF BUSYNESS

We live and work in a fast-paced, stress-riddled world. "Snail mail" has become our last resort. For matters of importance, we use email, overnight mail, faxes, text messages, and even notes on social media. Many of us devote hours each week simply reading and responding to emails, texting, and listening to voicemail. And this is before doing any *real* work!

It seems we have become the busiest generation of people in history. We're so busy perhaps we should no longer refer to the *business* world but rather, the *busy-ness* world. Technology has shrunk the globe in a practical sense, enabling the busy executive in Germany to instantly contact the equally busy leader in Mexico, for example, and increase their mutual busyness. A crisis in Japan can rapidly trigger an urgent situation for someone in the U.S.A.

Years ago I saw a sign that I considered adopting as a personal disclaimer: "Failure to plan on *your* part does not constitute an emergency on *my* part." A nice thought, but that's not always realistic. Unanticipated situations do occur that call for our immediate attention, whether we like it or not. So we just become busier.

But this business of busyness is hardly new. Decades ago, Mohandas Gandhi said, "There is more to life than merely increasing its speed." And author and thinker David Steindl-Rast observed, "The Chinese character or pictograph for 'busy' is composed of two characters: 'heart' and 'killing.'" Ponder that image for a moment!

So what's the solution? Do we adopt the attitude of the Broadway songwriter in the '60s who wrote, "Stop the World, I Want to Get Off"? At times that thought is tempting, but certainly hard to carry out – and probably not as desirable as it seems at first. At the same time, the prevailing mantra of so many people today, "We don't know where we're going, but we're making great time!" doesn't seem to work either. The answer, I believe, is seeking times of peace and calm in the midst of the busy and chaotic. Here are some insights from the Scriptures worth considering on this matter:

Plan well before taking action. In the midst of a crisis, the temptation is to respond quickly. "Do *something*, even if it's wrong!" But the truth is, if we didn't have time to do something right the first time, why is it we always seem to have time to do it over again? *"The plans of the diligent lead to profit as surely as haste leads to poverty"* (Proverbs 21:5).

Before doing something, be sure you know what you're doing – and where you're going. As we succumb to busyness, we tend to dive into projects, much like a swimmer who plunges into a pool without knowing what event she's competing in. It's often much better to stop, evaluate the magnitude of the task you're confronting, and determine whether you have all the information and resources necessary before proceeding. *"It is not good to have zeal without knowledge, nor to be hasty and miss the way"* (Proverbs 19:2).

Busyness may blind you to impending calamity. "Multi-tasking," studies have shown, is particularly hazardous while driving a car. Drivers preoccupied with cell phones, eating, texting, or jotting down reminder notes are accidents waiting to happen. The same is often true in the workplace. Are we so busy juggling many assignments and responsibilities we overlook major items that "slip through the cracks," to the detriment of ourselves and our companies? *"The prudent see danger and take refuge, but the simple keep going and suffer for it"* (Proverbs 27:12).

Before acting, pause and make God a part of the equation. The Bible asserts that God is as active and interested in what transpires in the workplace as He is in the sanctuary. Pausing long enough to seek His wisdom and guidance should never be regarded as a waste of time. *"Be still before the Lord and wait patiently before him…"* (Psalm 37:7).

PUTTING IT INTO PRACTICE

1. On a scale of 1 to 10, 1 being low and 10 being high, how busy would you say that you are? If you would rate yourself high on the scale, how did you get that way, and does it concern you at all? Why or why not?

    Conversely, if you would rank yourself low on the busyness scale, what's your secret in how you have achieved this?

2. What are some of the unique factors in your workplace that contribute to the level of busyness that you must deal with every day? Are there any things you can control – or at least influence – that could slow your hectic pace to a more manageable level?

3. Have you ever confronted a demanding situation that, in retrospect, caused you to wonder, "If we didn't have time to make certain it was done right the first time, why is it that we now have time to do it over again?" Give an example. How might you have proceeded differently at first, if given the opportunity?

4. Does it ever occur to you to pause before leaping into a project and consult God about how best to go about doing it? Do you think this does (or would) have any impact on your busyness and effectiveness? Why or why not?

CHAPTER 10

AVOIDING THE DOMINATING POWER OF MONEY

Dollars. Euros. Pesos. Yen. Forints. Reals. Rupies. Rubles. These are just some of the names used for currency around the world. No matter what you call it, it's the focus of much of our time, energy and attention: Money.

The daily news media give us stock market reports, economic analyses, price indexes and inflation projections. Financial officers develop budgets and maintain a vigilant watch over revenues and expenses. On a personal level, we study our checkbooks, savings accounts and investments, seeking to determine whether we will have sufficient funds for present and future needs.

In itself, money is neither good nor bad. However, we all have seen examples of the dominating force that money can have in people's lives. Marriages have been destroyed by unhealthy preoccupation with wealth and materialism. Careers have been ruined by the relentless quest of financial rewards. Some institutions have sacrificed their noble missions as they yielded to the whims and influences of substantial benefactors.

The Bible has as much to say about money as it does about any topic, and urges us to be extremely cautious about the power it can wield in our lives. In fact, in 1 Timothy 6:10 we're told, *"...the love of money is a root of all kinds of evil. Some people, eager for money, have wandered from the faith and pierced themselves with many griefs."* This does not mean money in itself is necessarily evil, but without question it can bring destructive consequences for anyone obsessed with acquiring and holding onto it. As you might imagine, Proverbs has many things to say about money. Here is just a sampling from its passages, exhorting us to be wise in our use of money:

Money can mislead. Someone has said, "Money is a good servant, but a dangerous master." Devoting our lives to the pursuit of riches may not result in the joy and fulfillment that we expect. *"The wicked man earns deceptive wages, but he who sows righteousness reaps a sure reward"* (Proverbs 11:18).

Money cannot buy strong moral character. When wealth becomes our goal, it becomes easy to make moral compromises to achieve that goal. Suddenly, "The end justifies the means." But you cannot put a price on solid character traits like integrity, generosity, love, compassion, loyalty and honesty. *"Whoever trusts in his riches will fall, but the righteous will thrive like a green leaf"* (Proverbs 11:28).

Money does not necessarily mean wealth. The wealthiest people are not always the ones who flaunt their possessions. Wealth need not be pretentious, and there is wealth – in terms of good works, kindness and selfless service – that cannot be measured on a balance sheet. *"One man pretends to be rich, yet has nothing; another pretends to be poor, yet has great wealth"* (Proverbs 13:7).

Money does not last. When you die, how much wealth will you leave behind? All of it! If we place our confidence in material wealth, inevitably it will betray our trust. It can undermine any positive impact we would hope to leave at the end of our lives. And when our time on earth is finished, we certainly cannot take our money and "stuff" with us. *"When a wicked man dies, his hope perishes; all he expected from his power comes to nothing"* (Proverbs 11:7). *"Do not wear yourself out to get rich; have the wisdom to show restraint. Cast but a glance at riches, and they are gone, for they will surely sprout wings and fly off to the sky like an eagle"* (Proverbs 23:4-5). *"...for riches do not endure forever, and a crown is not secure for all generations"* (Proverbs 27:24).

Money cannot solve all problems. The lack of money can cause an assortment of difficulties, but having money does not always solve them. In fact, possessing wealth can present an entirely different set of problems. We can agonize over how to avoid losing what we have. We can lose sleep worrying about how to acquire more. Just a taste of riches can stimulate an insatiable appetite for more money and things. *"Better a little with the fear of the Lord than great wealth with turmoil"* (Proverbs 15:16).

Putting It into Practice

1. How would you describe your attitude toward money? How much of your typical day is spent thinking about monetary concerns, whether at work or at home?

2. Do you believe, as the Bible states, that money is "a root of all kinds of evil"? What do you think that means, in a practical, everyday sense?

3. Can you think of an example, whether in your own life or in the life of someone you know, when inordinate concentration on money had disastrous consequences?

4. What steps do you think can be taken to avoid allowing money to become a dominating master? How can we maintain a perspective that money should be merely a tool, rather than a goal in itself?

CHAPTER 11

THE DREADFUL DELUSION OF DISHONESTY

D o you have any memories from childhood that, despite the passage of years, remain vividly etched in your mind? I have many, most of them good. But one memory comes to mind that, even though it seems relatively insignificant today, still makes me feel somewhat ashamed.

I was visiting with my grandfather in another city, and a new friend who was celebrating his birthday invited me to come over to his house that afternoon for a party. Being a big fan of ice cream and cake, I eagerly agreed. However, about an hour before the party, one of my aunts offered to take me to a bookstore and buy me a book as a gift. Since my appetite for books was stronger than for ice cream and cake, I conveniently "forgot" about the party, choosing not to mention it, and left with my aunt to get the new book.

Later, I lied to my friend, telling him that I had gotten confused about when the party was being held. He seemed to understand and forgave my absence, but deep down I felt guilty, knowing that out of selfishness I had deliberately chosen to be untruthful.

Decades later, I've learned many lessons about the virtues of honesty, especially in business. For instance, if I expect people to keep their commitments to me, I must be prepared to keep my commitments to them – even when it's not convenient. As noted earlier, honesty also is one of the foundation blocks for a good reputation. What takes a lifetime to build be destroyed in a moment of bad judgment or deceit. I could list other insights, but it probably would be far more valuable to consider what we can learn from principles we find presented in Proverbs:

Dishonest profits do not last. Sometimes it's tempting to lie in attempting to retain a client or win an account, but the danger is ever-present that the dishonesty will be exposed and any gains will quickly be forfeited. You won't need to fear being "exposed" if you tell the truth. *""A fortune made by a lying tongue is a fleeting vapor and a deadly snare"* (Proverbs 21:6) *"Truthful lips endure forever, but a lying tongue lasts only a moment"* (Proverbs 12:19).

Dishonest gains are not worth the "bad taste" of a seared conscience. I have encountered a few people who seem to have refined dishonesty into an art form, but for most of us, being untruthful is costly – to our self-esteem, conscience, and relationships. Being truthful does not carry such consequences. Consider this vivid analogy: *"Food gained by fraud tastes sweet to a man, but he ends up with a mouth full of gravel"* (Proverbs 20:17).

Dishonesty eventually will be discovered. An old saying warns us, "Your sins will find you out." Even if somehow you could manage to conceal dishonest actions and words throughout your lifetime, would you still want to risk having them exposed after your death? *"A false witness will not go unpunished, and he who pours out lies will not go free"* (Proverbs 19:5).

Dishonesty creates a wedge between ourselves and God. Even though our friends and associates may be unaware of our lies, if God is truly all-knowing as the Bible says He is, then He certainly knows. Do you really want to face His displeasure? *"The Lord detests differing weights, and dishonest scales do not please him"* (Proverbs 20:23 – see also Proverbs 12:22 and 20:10).

Honesty pleases others and wins their favor. When people know they can trust you and count on you for an honest reply, as well as honest behavior, you become someone they want to work with and spend time with. You gain their respect for your consistency by being straight-for-ward and reliable at all times. *"An honest answer is like a kiss on the lips"* (Proverbs 24:26).

Putting It into Practice

1. Have you ever worked with someone who habitually lied or at least distorted the truth for his or her benefit? How do you feel about that kind of person? If you needed to rely on them in a critical situation, would you be able to trust them?

2. On a scale of 1 to 10, how honest do you consider yourself to be? Have there been times when you were dishonest because it seemed in your best interest?

3. Has there ever been a situation in which you were caught in some form of dishonesty and had to suffer significant consequences? If so, why did you do it, and what happened? If the situation were to repeat itself, would you respond any differently now?

4. Do you think there are work environments that actually encourage dishonesty? If you were to find yourself in one of those settings, what do you think could be done to maintain your commitment to honesty in what you say and do? Or would you simply yield to the prevailing "culture"?

CHAPTER 12

ARE YOU WHOLEHEARTED, OR ONLY HALF-HEARTED?

The story is told about the little boy who was misbehaving at the family dinner table. "Billy, sit down and be quiet!" his father demanded. Reluctantly, Billy sat down, but after a few moments he announced to all within earshot, "I'm sitting down on the outside, but I'm standing up on the inside!"

Have you ever felt like that? When I was young, there were times when my father or mother would ask me to do some little task or chore that I did not want to do. Being a generally obedient child, I might voice a word of complaint, but then proceed to do as I had been told. However, often I would make it clear through my attitude and actions that my heart was really not in what I was doing. I suspect there were many times when I seemed very much like that little boy at the dinner table.

You don't have to be a child to act this way, however. It happens every day in the workplace as well. Executives and managers direct employees on assignments for them to perform, then the employees either do the work, grumbling the entire time, or only give the job a half-hearted effort because they don't agree with what needs to be done – or how it should be accomplished.

I admit I've been guilty of this myself at times. Bosses are not perfect – they make mistakes and err in judgment – but that doesn't release us from carrying out our workplace responsibilities to the best of our abilities. A verse from the Bible addresses this well. Colossians 3:17 urges,

"And whatever you do, whether in word or deed, do it all in the name of the Lord Jesus...." As a follower of Christ, the things I do – and how I do them – reflect on my relationship with God. The book of Proverbs offers additional insights, showing how motives and attitudes are just as important as our actions. Consider the following:

It's not just what you do, but why you do it. When you do an act of kindness, or put in extra effort in a project, why do you do it? Is it because you know that it's the right thing to do, or because you expect to gain recognition – or possible rewards, or advancement – for doing it? Be careful of ulterior motives – doing things that look good outwardly, but inwardly are motivated from a desire for some form of personal gain. *"All a man's ways seem innocent to him, but motives are weighed by the Lord"* (Proverbs 16:2).

You can deceive yourself with your actions. Have you ever done something that down deep you knew was wrong, or at least questionable, but were able to rationalize it and convince yourself that the action was acceptable – even desirable? Convincing ourselves that something is right may salve our conscience, but it does not necessarily make it right. *"All a man's ways seem right to him, but the Lord weighs the heart"* (Proverbs 21:2).

Circumstances can reveal where your heart is. What happens when your actions don't bring about the expected results? How do you respond? If you become angry, spiteful or discouraged, that could provide clear evidence that your heart and motives were not as pure as you thought they were, or as you led other people to believe. *"The crucible for silver and the furnace for gold, but the Lord tests the heart"* (Proverbs 17:3).

Be willing to admit those times when you have been half-hearted. As much as we would like to think our motives are always pure and noble, and that we pursue each task wholeheartedly, there inevitably will be times when this isn't true. When we realize this, we can ignore the truth, expending great effort to defend why we acted in such a way, or can simply admit our failure and strive to do better the next time. At the same time, we need not delay necessary and desired action until we are certain that our motivations are absolutely pure. In that case, we might not get much done at all! *"Who can say, 'I have kept my heart pure; I am clean and without sin'?"* (Proverbs 20:9).

PUTTING IT INTO PRACTICE

1. Do you ever stop to evaluate your motives for what you are doing – or not doing? Explain your answer.

2. Would you agree with the premise of this chapter that why we do things is as important as whether, and how, we do them? Why or why not?

3. Read Colossians 3:17 again. Think of a time when you were less than wholehearted in carrying out some responsibility or assignment. Can you explain the situation, and why you acted with less than total commitment and enthusiasm?

4. How do you think it might be possible to avoid being half-hearted in the things we do and in the relationships we form with other people? How might a strong relationship with God influence your approach to work and your interactions with people?

CHAPTER 13

DISCIPLINE: THE 'REWARD' NOBODY LIKES

Even though we humans are by far the most complex and sophisticated organisms on Earth, there are still valuable truths and principles we can learn from other realms of nature. Consider the plant world, for example. Have you ever tried to grow tomatoes, roses, or grapes? While those plants are very different, they all share one common need: To be "trained," so they grow properly. Without some kind of supporting framework to keep them off the ground and enable them to grow upward and outward, none of these plants will be very productive. However, with proper support and nurture, they all will bear rich, ripe fruit or beautiful, delicate flowers.

Another term we could use for such botanical "training" is *discipline* – applying specific methods to ensure that they grow according to their design. Applying this principle to young people, Proverbs 22:6 says, *"Train a child in the way he should go...."* Discipline is also an important concept in the world of work. It requires discipline to arrive for work each day on time. Discipline prompts us to devote the necessary time and energy to complete a difficult task or project. And discipline motivates us to acquire the necessary knowledge, training and skills to perform our jobs more effectively and efficiently.

However, at times discipline must be imposed upon us by other sources – such as a supervisor, or a mentor. Like a tomato plant that needs to be fastened onto a stick or another form of support so it will grow properly, someone with authority over us may need to discipline us so we can grow properly in our jobs.

Unfortunately, we do not always respond to discipline easily. If we have worked hard on a project, it can be hard being corrected, told that it wasn't performed in a satisfactory manner. Maybe an element of our behavior in interacting with peers and coworkers needs improvement. Or a mentor might point to an area of our lives that needs to be changed or adjusted. How we respond to such correction – or discipline – can greatly affect our future success. Consider some of what the book of Proverbs has to say about discipline:

Our response to discipline influences others. If you aspire to be an effective leader, be aware that people will be watching how you respond to every situation – including how you react when being the recipient of discipline. *"He who heeds discipline shows the way to life, but whoever ignores correction leads others astray"* (Proverbs 10:17).

The wise person appreciates discipline. It may bruise our egos or deflate our pride to be informed that something we have done is not acceptable, or that an area of our work performance requires improvement. But we would be wise to understand this correction, no matter how unpleasant, is for our ultimate good. Therefore, we should receive the needed discipline with humility and gratitude. *"Whoever loves discipline loves knowledge, but he who hates correction is stupid"* (Proverbs 12:1).

There are rewards to be gained through discipline. At first, being corrected seems like a setback. However, discipline may well result in our becoming a better salesperson, a more effective administrator, or a more valued leader. If we regard discipline as a means to enhance and strengthen our abilities and skills, we will become better for it. *"He who scorns instruction will pay for it, but he who respects a command is rewarded"* (Proverbs 13:13).

We demonstrate concern for others through discipline. A good leader will not allow a worker to continue to perform in a substandard manner. Instead, the leader cares enough – about the individual and his organization – to teach and demonstrate how to properly and acceptably carry out an assignment. It's an essential part of an effective overall strategy for developing the individual. *"He who spares the rod hates his son, but he who loves him is careful to discipline him"* (Proverbs 13:24).

The greatest failure is rejecting discipline. Arrogance and destructive pride manifest themselves in people who refuse to be corrected when work or behavior is out of line. Such resistance may eventually result in great loss – of a job, of personal possessions, and even of one's hopes and dreams. *"He who ignores discipline despises himself, but whoever heeds correction gains understanding"* (Proverbs 15:32).

Putting It into Practice

1. Can you think of other examples found in nature that teach the importance of discipline – of being properly trained? When you have looked at a grapevine, or a rosebush, has the concept of discipline ever come to your mind?

2. If you are a parent, what is your approach to discipline? How did your own parents discipline you when you were young – were they harsh and overbearing, or did they discipline you appropriately with love and sensitivity?

3. How do you typically respond when you're being disciplined? Why?

4. Think of some ways discipline has helped you in your career? Explain specifically how it has enhanced you personally and the work that you do.

CHAPTER 14

SPIRITUALITY AND THE WORKPLACE

We spend many of our waking hours in the tangible, material, bottom line-driven environment we call the business and professional world. Many of us assume the attitude of, "If you can't see it or hold it, it doesn't matter." Yet more and more, the value and importance of the unseen and intangible is being affirmed – even for hard-charging business people.

Prominent business publications are recognizing that spirituality has a legitimate place in the marketplace of the 21st century. For instance, one issue of *Business Week* featured the cover story, "Religion in the Workplace." An edition of *FORTUNE* magazine carried the title, "God and Business." Many other publications, including the *Wall Street Journal* and *Forbes,* also have seriously considered the link between spirituality and the workplace.

There are many explanations for this relatively new phenomenon. It may involve a growing awareness and understanding that we are not merely physical, intellectual and emotional beings – that we also possess an innate spiritual dimension. In the chaotic, unpredictable world of business, many are searching for a source of stability, a sense of meaning, and answers for some of life's ultimate questions. And a medical publication I read recently declared that scientific studies have shown spirituality can help to promote mental and physical health, with benefits such as lower blood pressure, enhanced immune systems, recovery from substance abuse, and faster recuperation from surgeries and illness.

However, many of these articles also underscore the importance of distinguishing between religion (typically viewed in terms of formalized structure, rituals, traditions, dogma and exclusivity) and spirituality, which is regarded as intensely personal, involving a relationship with God (or a "higher power"), other people, and even the world around us. As one CEO commented in an article published by the *MIT Sloan Management Review*, "I believe strongly that religion should not be discussed in the workplace. On the other hand, I believe not only that spirituality can be discussed…but that its discussion is absolutely key if we are to create and maintain ethical, truly caring organizations."

Discovering a connection between spirituality and both personal and professional well-being, however, is hardly new. Consider, for example, some of the insights about this reality as presented in the timeless book of Proverbs:

Spirituality offers principles worth following. In a world where so many people contend there is no such thing as "absolute truth," spirituality counters by insisting that there are valid, eternal standards and guidelines for everyday conduct. *"The highway of the upright avoids evil; he who guards his way guards his life"* (Proverbs 16:17).

Spirituality provides a sense of security and safety. Whether our concern is global terrorism or concerns about how our company can survive competitive pressures, we long for something – or Someone – to serve as a source of hope and reassurance in the face of extreme uncertainty. True spirituality can fill that need. *"He who fears the Lord has a secure fortress, and for his children it will be a refuge"* (Proverbs 14:26). *"The name of the Lord is a strong tower; the righteous run to it and are safe"* (Proverbs 18:10).

Spirituality nurtures an attitude of peace and contentment. The day-to-day challenges we face in the business and professional world can create a state of high anxiety, but a life anchored in deep spiritual convictions can help to minimize such stress and pressure. *"The fear of the Lord leads to life; then one rests content, untouched by trouble"* (Proverbs 19:23).

Spirituality becomes a source of wisdom and direction. When seeking guidance for the difficult decisions we face each day, the truths and principles we find through spiritual pursuits can point us to much-needed solutions. *"He holds victory in store for the upright, he is a shield to those whose walk is blameless, for he guards the course of the just and protects the way of his faithful ones"* (Proverbs 2:7-8). *"He who trusts in himself is a fool, but he who walks in wisdom is kept safe"* (Proverbs 28:26).

PUTTING IT INTO PRACTICE

1. When you think of "spirituality," what comes to your mind? Do you agree with the distinction between spirituality and religion made by the business leader in the *MIT Sloan Management Review* article? Why or why not?

2. How do you view yourself in terms of spirituality – do you consider yourself to be a spiritual person, or someone who has significant interest in spirituality? Explain your answer.

3. Do you agree that spirituality has a legitimate place and role in the business and professional world? Tell how you have reached your conclusion.

4. Which – if any – of the insights from Proverbs on spirituality seem most interesting or meaningful to you? How can you see them being applied to your present workplace situation?

CHAPTER 15

THE GREATEST PROBLEM IN THE BUSINESS WORLD

How would you answer if someone were to ask what you considered to be the greatest, most pervasive problem in the business and professional world today? Some people might respond that it's dishonesty. Some might single out greed as the greatest problem. Others might say that it's a general lack of integrity. And still others might believe jealousy or envy is the most troublesome problem. Lack of compassion and sensitivity also result in problems that often raise their ugly heads. You can probably think of other candidates for the "honor" of *"Greatest Problem in the Business World Today."*

Each area mentioned above is certainly a significant instigator of problems. But I would suggest a far greater problem, one that could be regarded as the underlying cause of all of the others that we have listed.

This problem is simple, yet profound: *PRIDE.* C.S. Lewis, a renowned British author, university professor and one of the 20th century's greatest thinkers, stated, "There is one vice of which no man in the world is free; which everyone in the world loathes when he sees it in someone else; and of which hardly any people…ever imagine that they are guilty themselves…. The vice I am talking of is Pride or Self-Conceit…. Pride leads to every other vice: it is the complete anti-God state of mind."

Lewis originally wrote this more than 70 years ago in a chapter called "The Great Sin" in his book, *Mere Christianity.* (If you have never read it, it's worth the time and investment.) Today, in the 21st century, the problem has not changed. If anything, it has intensified. We see the evidence – and devastation – of pride in every area of life: business, politics, education, sports, medicine, religion, entertainment, marriage and the family. According to the Bible, it gave birth to all the problems of mankind and remains an uncontained, destructive force.

Several thousands of years ago, long before C.S. Lewis would make his bold statement, the book of Proverbs also presented some serious observations about pride and its bitter consequences. Consider the following:

Pride produces conflict. We all have gotten involved in disputes where the central issue became one person's insistence on proving he or she was right, regardless of the facts. These are never enjoyable, and rarely very productive, especially when the other people involved in the conflict are equally prideful. It quickly declines into a lose-lose situation. *"Pride only breeds quarrels, but wisdom is found in those who take advice"* (Proverbs 13:10).

Pride can cause one's downfall. We have heard and read about so many top executives that have ruined major corporations and organizations – and their careers – by selfish manipulation of people, funds and stockholder reports that it hardly seems like news anymore. We can enumerate many specifics regarding their legendary and notorious falls. But be assured, pride is at the root of these horrendous leadership failures, in one way or another. *"Pride goes before destruction, a haughty spirit before a fall"* (Proverbs 16:18).

Pride reflects the state of a person's inner self. As Lewis wrote, we all hate to see pride in someone else because we recognize it for what it is: self-centeredness and conceit, rather than selfless concern for others. But as has been often stated, whenever we point a finger toward someone else's flaws, our other fingers point toward ourselves. So we must be honest about our own susceptibility to prideful thinking and actions. *"Haughty eyes and a proud heart, the lamp of the wicked, are sin!"* (Proverbs 21:4).

Pride's antidote is humility. Just as we dislike obvious displays of pride, humility is a trait we all admire – even if we do not fully understand it. Mohandas Gandhi and Mother Teresa were just two examples of leaders who modeled this quality. Rather than promoting self, it may be a revelation to discover that our goals can be best realized through unselfish consideration of the needs and concerns of others. *"The fear of the Lord teaches a man wisdom, and humility comes before honor"* (Proverbs 15:33).

Putting It into Practice

1. Give an example of someone you know – perhaps a person you work with (or work for) – who has an obvious problem with pride? How does it make you feel to be around people like this?

2. Do you agree with C.S. Lewis's assessment that pride is "one vice of which no man in the world is free"? Explain your answer. If you are in agreement with Lewis, how does this problem of pride exhibit itself in your own life?

3. If pride is truly a matter of the heart, how does a person overcome this problem? Are there instances when pride is acceptable – even desirable? Explain your answer.

4. Earlier we considered examples of people who exhibit excessive pride to the detriment of themselves and those around them. Contrast this with someone you know personally who consistently displays genuine humility? If so, describe this person and tell how you think the individual has been able to cultivate this admirable trait.

CHAPTER 16

WHICH WAY SHOULD I GO?

Recently I heard from a good friend who told me he had resigned from his job, effective at the end of the previous year. He didn't know what he would be doing next, but felt strongly that to continue at his current place of employment would be a disservice to himself and to his employer. He had some savings he could live on for a time, but most important, wanted to give himself an opportunity to stop and re-evaluate the direction of his life and his vocational future.

This requires a step of faith, as well as courage and integrity. Most of us would hang onto our present positions until we had secured better employment. At times, that's exactly what I have done. But my friend, who has been growing not only professionally but also spiritually for more than 10 years, isn't willing to settle for less than God's best for himself and his family. The question is, how can he determine what in fact *is* God's best for him and what direction he should take for the next years of his life?

One of the things I have come to appreciate so much about the Bible is its practicality. It offers sound, meaningful principles for everyday life – even our work – as well as eternal life. These principles have been invaluable for me and many people I know. It seems any time we're beginning new pursuits that present unseen opportunities and challenges, it's a good time to learn (or relearn) how best to discern the proper direction for our lives, as well as to answer the question we are likely to face many times: "Which way should I go?"

Don't always rely on what seems to be obvious. Sometimes it's impossible to recognize what lies ahead, like being unable to see a person approaching from around the corner of a building. It's also a bit like following directions for traveling in an area where we have never been before: We simply must trust the guidance we have received is correct and that it will take us to our intended destination. *"We live by faith, not by sight"* (2 Corinthians 5:7).

Don't expect to understand everything that happens. We may experience an unexpected setback, or an obstacle may suddenly impede our ability to reach an important goal. Even our more carefully planned presentations may fail to yield the desired outcomes, despite our very best efforts. At times like these, it's reassuring to believe God is fully capable of turning apparent defeat into victory. *"Trust in the Lord with all your heart and lean not on your own understanding; in all your ways acknowledge him, and he will make your paths straight"* (Proverbs 3:5,6).

Try to be honest about your motives. Sometimes the decisions we make can be shaped, or at least influenced, by faulty reasoning. We can respond impulsively out of pride, anger or frustration. The best interests of everyone involved may become obscured by improper motives. Understandably, the result can be disastrous, so before taking an important step, be certain to ask yourself, "Why am I doing this?" *"All a man's ways seem right to him, but the Lord weighs the heart"* (Proverbs 21:2).

Before taking action, seek out reliable advice. In trying to evaluate our lives, we cannot help but have a biased perspective, based on our past experiences and future expectations. In various ways, we may be too close to the situation to consider it objectively. Many times it's helpful, therefore, to solicit impartial advice and counsel from knowledgeable people who can provide needed objectivity and offer different and insightful points of view. We may not always like what they have to say, but at least they can help us to recognize how things really are, rather than how we want them to be. *"Where there is no guidance the people fall, but in abundance of counselors there is victory"* (Proverbs 11:14, NAS).

PUTTING IT INTO PRACTICE

1. When you are confronted with a difficult decision, somewhat at a loss as to what you should do or what direction you should take, what typically is your first course of action?

2. How do you feel about the idea of "living by faith, not by sight"? Is that a scary thought, not wanting to deal with the feeling of not being in control? Can you think of other aspects of everyday life that, like it or not, we must accept by faith, without solid, objective proof?

3. Can you think of any circumstances that seemed difficult, even impossible, to understand at the time, but in retrospect you were able to see the reason for them – at least to some degree? Describe one such situation, if you can.

4. Why is it that our hearts, our motives, can prove troublesome as we seek direction at critical junctures of our lives? Do you have at least one person that you trust enough who can help you in honestly evaluating your motivations as you try to reach important – perhaps even life-changing – decisions?

CHAPTER 17

CRITICISM: CRUCIAL, CARING COMMUNICATION

For years I have subscribed to this motto: "I wouldn't mind pain... if it didn't hurt so much!" I hold a similar regard for criticism. I have great awareness of my many imperfections, but still I'm not fond of having them pointed out to me. Stating it another way, criticism wouldn't be so bad – if it wasn't painful to receive it.

In my organization, we use an excellent personal assessment tool called the Birkman Method that evaluates an individual in many areas. One of its 11 primary components is called "Esteem," which measures a person's sensitivity in relating to individuals – particularly those he or she holds in high regard. People with a high Esteem "need" have a deep-down yearning for affirmation and praise. Some people call it receiving "attaboys." When negative comments outweigh the positives, it can put them into stress, causing them to withdraw from interacting with others, become overly sensitive, or feel discouraged. People like this rarely welcome criticism, at least not without an equal or greater serving of praise.

Regardless of where we fall on the "Esteem" scale, most of us do not *enjoy* receiving criticism. But often it can be the most crucial, caring and constructive service anyone could do for us. When I was 16, I spent some weeks with my uncle and aunt in another city. He took me under his wing, teaching me some important lessons, including the value of hard work and initiative. Until then, I must admit, I had been a fairly unmotivated, take-life-as-it-happens teenager. My uncle's criticism – communicated to me in an affirming manner – was pivotal for my development as a young person starting to look ahead toward college and a career.

Criticism can enhance our professional careers in many ways. Well-intended correction can aid us in making favorable first impressions, whether interviewing for a new job or meeting with a new client. We might undertake a project thinking we have done it properly, but a critique from a wiser, more experienced coworker, explaining how it could be improved, can enhance our future performance. Most of us aren't naturally skilled public speakers, so criticism and advice from someone whose insights we value can sharpen our oral presentations.

The problem occurs when we resist, or even resent, criticism meant for our good. We might respond by thinking, "Who do they think they are, saying that? They can't tell me what to do!" We all have probably reacted this way at one time or another. Such a response is hardly a new phenomenon. In fact, the ancient book of Proverbs – the "book of wisdom" – offers many observations about criticism, referring to it as "rebuke" or correction:

Corrective criticism. Which would you rather receive: stern words pointing out areas of your professional performance that need to be changed, or severe punishment for failure to correct the undesirable behavior? *"A rebuke impresses a man of discernment more than a hundred lashes a fool"* (Proverbs 17:10).

Treasures in criticism. Even when it's hard to accept, criticism usually contains at least an element of truth. We are wise to consider it carefully before dismissing it. *"He who listens to a life-giving rebuke will be at home among the wise"* (Proverbs 15:31).

The gift of criticism. An adage states, "If you can't say something nice, don't say anything at all." But if your constructive criticism would bring benefit to another person, electing to withhold your comments would be unkind and inconsiderate. *"He who rebukes a man will in the end gain more favor than he who has a flattering tongue"* (Proverbs 28:23).

Penalty of unheeded criticism. Even though it might seem painful, wise and caring criticism might offer the only escape from potentially devastating and irreversible consequences. We are wise to pay attention. *"A man who remains stiff-necked after many rebukes will suddenly be destroyed – without remedy"* (Proverbs 29:1).

PUTTING IT INTO PRACTICE

1. How do you typically react to criticism? Why do you think you respond in this way?

2. Can you think of a time when criticism seemed unwarranted and without merit, but afterward you realized how much you needed to hear it and appreciated that someone had cared enough to tell you?

3. What are some ways criticism can be communicated effectively, without causing unnecessary harm to a person's ego or self-esteem? Should that even be a consideration? Why or why not?

4. What steps can you take so that the next time someone offers criticism, even if expressed in a harsh or insensitive manner, you will receive it more readily?

CHAPTER 18

INTEGRITY: ONE SAFEGUARD
AGAINST DISASTER

The story is told about a farmer who left his prized cow with a friend so he could go on a trip for several days. The cow died while the farmer was gone, and he was distraught to learn the sad news upon his return.

"I was going to sell the cow," he said. "I desperately need the money." Then he decided, "I will still sell the cow – by lottery." He sold 300 tickets at $2 each, and presented the dead cow to the winner of the lottery. When the winner complained that he had no use for a dead cow, the farmer apologized and returned the $2 for his ticket - and retained the remaining $598!

This is one picture of what has been occurring in the business world, particularly in the technology industry. Instead of bricks and mortar, investors have become shareholders in ideas, dreams – and unfortunately in some cases, ill-intended schemes. In the wonderful vision of hindsight, many people – especially venture capitalists – are discovering too late that they have been buying stock in dead cows.

Reports of ethical misconduct within major corporations have caused turmoil in the world's stock markets, anxiety and anger among shareholders, and general distrust for once-highly esteemed companies and their top leaders. How could such acts of corporate mismanagement occur – and how could business leaders, who should know better, knowingly carry them out?

There are many reasons: greed, pride, lack of accountability, deceit-fulness, defiance of ethical standards (or simply ignoring or denying that such clear standards even exist). Each of these is a topic worthy of its own chapter, but let me suggest another probable cause: failure within the business and professional community at large to recognize the incalculable, irreplaceable value of *integrity*.

The measure of a good leader is not limited to just what he or she accomplishes in terms of a balance sheet; even more important is the depth of their personal character. And there is no character quality more essential for good leadership than integrity.

But integrity is much more than merely a preferred virtue. It serves as one certain way of protecting against disaster – personally and corpo-rately. Consider some of the things that the book of Proverbs has to say about integrity:

A person of integrity need not fear the truth. If you insist on sticking with the facts and what is true, you won't have to worry about remember-ing your lies. Falsehoods have an annoying way of revealing themselves at most unexpected – and inopportune – times. *"The man of integrity walks securely, but he who takes crooked paths will be found out"* (Proverbs 10:9).

Failure to act with integrity results in devastation. In a similar sense, the truth of any situation has an uncanny way of making itself known, sooner or later. People of integrity can sleep soundly, untroubled by the fear of becoming "found out" by the truth. *"The integrity of the upright guides them, but the unfaithful are destroyed by their duplicity"* (Proverbs 11:3).

Consequences of acting without integrity are widespread. Misdeeds at the highest levels of corporations have had an impact far beyond the companies and individuals involved. The entire business world has been affected, and individual consumers and investors have become unwit-ting victims of the resulting economic devastation. *"By justice a king gives country stability, but one who is greedy for bribes tears it down"* (Proverbs 29:4).

Protect integrity as you would a prized heirloom. Would you make a game of tossing around a piece of valuable china or priceless crystal? Of course not. If you or the person you throw it to were to drop it, it would become broken far beyond repair. The same applies to our personal integrity, which is a foundational element of our personal reputation. *"If you argue your case with a neighbor, do not betray another man's confidence, or he who hears it may shame you and you will never lose your bad reputation"* (Proverbs 25:9-10).

PUTTING IT INTO PRACTICE

1. Have you – or has someone you know – ever been asked to invest in something that ultimately amounted to something similar to a "dead cow," as described in the opening story? How did you feel when you discovered you had been deceived? Would you do business with that person again?

2. Do you agree that integrity is, or should be, an essential trait possessed by a person put into an important leadership role? Why or why not?

3. How would you define *integrity,* and how would you go about identifying it in someone you work for, or who works for you?

4. What are the benefits of striving to live and work according to a high standard of integrity? Can you think of any downsides to that? Explain.

    Why do you think that in the business and professional world overall, integrity often seems in short supply?

CHAPTER 19

NO MANURE, NO MILK!

Have you ever told yourself something like, "My job would be great if it were not for all the problems I have to deal with!"? If thoughts like this have ever crossed your mind, you are an unofficial member of a club with many millions of members. In fact, you would be hard-pressed to find anyone who does not belong to this "distinguished" society of problem-bemoaners.

More than 200 years ago, Scottish poet Robert Burns wrote, "The best laid schemes o' mice and men gang aft agley," which paraphrased means that even our best-considered, most carefully arranged plans often fail. We diligently plan for the coming day, trying to anticipate any and all obstacles that could interfere with the accomplishment of our objectives. Then we arrive at work with enthusiasm and optimism overflowing. But before our first cup of coffee starts to cool, something happens that spoils or at least complicates our meticulous plans.

It might be an emergency that interrupts the schedule, dramatically affecting the course of the day. Perhaps much-needed research being gathered at another office is late in arriving, or does not arrive at all. Maybe your computer freezes up and the work you just had to finish must be put on hold until some tech-savvy savior can arrive to analyze and correct the problem. You may have to intervene in a dispute between two or more staff members. Or it could be something as simple as spilling that initial cup of coffee on the report you must present at a meeting set to commence in 15 minutes.

There seems to be no end to the types of problems that can instantly transform a workday from calm to chaotic. If only there were some way to eliminate such difficulties, right? Perhaps our companies could provide us with "Easy Fix" buttons, similar to those that have appeared in commercials for a prominent office products retailer.

Amazingly enough, attempting to eliminate all workplace dilemmas might not be wise. Problems we encounter in the working environment – as well as our personal lives – often prove to be necessary (albeit annoying) ingredients to the success of our endeavors. Just as the wood of a tree becomes stronger when the tree is forced to endure harsh weather conditions, our overall performance can be enhanced as we learn to properly respond to challenging problems, both expected and unanticipated.

A key employee, for example, may have a less than appealing personality. Yet that individual's skills and expertise might greatly outweigh the inconvenience and unpleasantness involved in dealing with his or her quirks. Sometimes the people that seem most prone to rub against us like sandpaper end up serving a noble purpose, that of smoothing out some of our own rough edges.

In reality, problems can prove beneficial in many ways. Here are just two of them, according to the book of Proverbs:

No manure, no milk. Years ago, a friend was taking part in a high-level meeting to discuss whether his city should host a major international event. Much of the meeting focused on the many potential problems that could result if masses of people from different cultures converged upon the city. The overall tone of the meeting, to that point, had become decidedly negative. However, when my friend finally was asked to offer his perspective on the opportunity, he simply quoted Proverbs 14:4, which says, *"Where there are no oxen, the manger is empty, but from the strength of an ox comes an abundant harvest."* In other words, no manure, no milk! To express this insight yet another way, "If you want the benefits, you have to be willing to deal with the messes that come with it."

Strength through stress. Anyone can enjoy a measure of success when things go easily, as planned, and on schedule. But the true measures of both skill and character are shown by how we cope with and respond to the trials we must confront over the course of an ordinary day. Do we tailspin into a panic, frustrated by having our best-laid plans disrupted, or do we carefully assess the situation, weigh the options and determine what would be the best course for overcoming the problem? Do we contribute to the chaos, or convey and help to cultivate a sense of calm despite the surrounding storm? *"If you falter in times of trouble, how small is your strength!"* (Proverbs 24:10)

Putting It into Practice

1. What kind of problems do you regularly face in your job? Do you approach them with confidence, eager to work to resolve them, or do you struggle with them, simply wishing they would disappear?

2. Think of a specific time when you thought you had the day carefully planned, only to have it fall apart in the face of unexpected events. What was it like? How did you respond to it?

3. Can you relate to the admonition, "no manure, no milk," or is this a new insight for you? Explain.

4. Do you see a need for some changes in how you typically react when unexpected problems arise? How could you learn to regard them as opportunities to excel, rather than as causes for panic?

CHAPTER 20

THE INCREDIBLE IMPACT OF A TIMELY WORD

When I was a boy, I often heard other children declare, "Sticks and stones may break my bones, but names will never hurt me!" That sounded good at the time, but as I've matured it has become evident that words have far greater potential for inflicting pain than blunt objects.

That certainly does not make the throwing of stones or sticks acceptable, but if you really want to hurt someone, just say something cruel, insensitive, or vindictive. The sound of hearing another person call you "stupid" or "worthless," or say something like, "I hate you. Nobody likes you," will continue to echo and cause pain much longer than the agony of receiving a physical blow.

The Bible refers to the tongue as "a fire, a world of evil among the parts of the body" (James 3:6). It can scar emotions, causing damage beyond measure. But the same tongue – when used discerningly and constructively – can become an instrument of exquisite healing and encouragement. A few kind words can miraculously transform a dismal day in the workplace into a time of hope and enthusiasm. I can think of numerous times when an oppressive mood of discouragement or anxiety was dispelled when someone took the time to stop by my office or call me on the phone simply to express a few words of appreciation or sincere concern.

It's interesting to note that the book of Proverbs recognizes and places great emphasis on the potential benefit – and harm – that can result from the spoken word. Dozens of verses are devoted to the words that come out of our mouths and how they are presented. Here is just a sampling of the principles Proverbs teaches about our everyday speech:

Words can be used to hurt or to heal. Work pressures can cause us to speak harshly or carelessly, inflicting pain on those who are the targets of our words. But carefully chosen words, offered at the right time and in the right spirit, can be like a soothing balm. *"Reckless words pierce like a sword, but the tongue of the wise brings healing"* (Proverbs 12:18).

Words can promote self-preservation or bring about self-destruction. Those helped or harmed by the words we speak are not only our hearers – our words also have an impact on ourselves. *"He who guards his lips guards his life, but he who speaks rashly will come to ruin"* (Proverbs 13:3).

Words can bring peace or incite chaos. It is amazing how even the simplest words can either ease the emotion of the moment or escalate tension into conflict. *"A gentle answer turns away wrath, but a harsh word stirs up anger"* (Proverbs 15:1).

There is nothing better than words expressed in a timely, appropriate manner. Wise people recognize the power of words and use them to lift up the spirits of people around them. *"A man finds joy in giving an apt reply – and how good is a timely word!"* (Proverbs 15:23).

There is wisdom in remaining silent. A great statesman once said, "It is better to keep quiet and be thought a fool than to speak and remove all doubt." The writer of Proverbs agrees: *"Even a fool is thought wise if he keeps silent, and discerning if he holds his tongue"* (Proverbs 17:28).

Consider your words before releasing them. In the heat of the moment, we all are tempted to say things we might later regret. It does no harm to pause and carefully consider the potential impact of our words before we use them. *"The heart of the righteous weighs its answers, but the mouth of the wicked gushes evil"* (Proverbs 15:28).

Truthful words are an asset. There are those who do not appreciate honesty; they prefer to be told what they want to hear. But speaking the truth in an understanding, respectful manner wins far more friends than enemies. *"Kings take pleasure in honest lips; they value a man who speaks the truth"* (Proverbs 16:13).

PUTTING IT INTO PRACTICE

1. What kind of speaker are you: Do you say what you are thinking and wait until later to assess the consequences, or do you think carefully before you speak?

   Can you think of a specific time when you spoke hastily and then wished that you could retrieve your words?

2. Can you remember a time when someone said something that hurt you deeply? How did you respond? Can you sometimes still feel the sting of those words?

3. Which of the principles cited from the passages in Proverbs seems most meaningful for you?

5. What steps could be taken in your workplace to encourage people (including yourself) to speak more positively and constructively to one another? What could be the impact of this – both in terms of relationships between individuals and the atmosphere of the business overall?

CHAPTER 21

THERE IS NO SATISFYING THE NEEDS OF GREED

An incredibly wealthy businessman was asked by a news reporter, "How much is enough?" Without blinking an eye, the industrial mogul candidly replied with a smile, "Just a little bit more."

You have to give this man credit – at least he was honest. Basically he was confirming what we all know: No matter how much you have, or how little, there is always the temptation to yearn for "a little bit more." It would seem logical that there should be a point when a person, especially someone who is very affluent, would be able to say, "All right. That's enough. I have all that I need, and there is no sense in striving for more." But I have never met a person who said this and truly meant it. Have you?

There is a simple word for this problem: Greed. Certainly it has been a factor in the highly publicized ethical scandals surrounding some of the world's most prominent executives. Professional athletes sign unbelievably huge contracts, only to voice their displeasure soon afterward when they discover a rival player has just negotiated a deal guaranteeing a higher salary than they will receive.

But greed knows no cultural, class, or economic boundaries. You don't have to be fabulously rich to be controlled by greed. We work hard, receive a promotion and a pay increase, and feel content. That contentment is fleeting, however. It may last for a day, a week or two, even a month. But then we start wondering what it would be like to be earning even more money. We may confine our grumbling to ourselves, or express to others that we do not feel appreciated. Or we might start looking for another job, one that would pay us "what we deserve." Greed is a vicious cycle that never stops spinning.

What are some of the consequences of greed when it is left unchecked? Consider the following observations on this subject from the ancient but ever-contemporary book of Proverbs:

Greed diminishes life rather than building it. When "more" becomes our consuming desire, the focal point of our every waking moment, we can easily start to lose touch with reality. Many of the joys in life, those that cannot be measured or assigned monetary values, can be disregarded or lost in the ceaseless quest for material gain. *"Such is the end of all who go after ill-gotten gain; it takes away the lives of those who get it"* (Proverbs 1:19).

Greed destroys relationships. What value can you put on a loving smile, a cheerful greeting, a warm hug or an intimate embrace? When we let ourselves become overwhelmed by greed and the pursuit of "just a little bit more," we may not be available to receive such priceless gifts when they present themselves. Healthy, growing relationships don't come with price tags, but the cost of losing them is great. How much warmth and comfort can you receive from hugging a bank statement, or a stuffed wallet? *"A greedy man brings trouble to his family, but he who hates bribes will live"* (Proverbs 15:27).

Greed distorts our focus. The greedy person spends many waking hours scheming how to acquire more, but fails to understand and appreciate the incomparable joys and intangible advantages of giving rather than receiving. When the focus is on self, the needs of others are easily overlooked or dismissed. *"All day long he craves for more, but the righteous give without sparing"* (Proverbs 21:26).

Greed deceives at the end. Shortly after the death of the man who admitted he wanted "just a little bit more," his financial adviser was asked how much the rich industrialist had left behind. The answer was brief but profound: "He left it all!" If we can't take it with us, if all we have strived for and sacrificed to acquire is lost the moment we take our final breath, is it really worth all the effort we have expended to accumulate so much and hold onto it? *"Death and Destruction are never satisfied, and neither are the eyes of man"* (Proverbs 27:20).

PUTTING IT INTO PRACTICE

1. Do you personally struggle with greed? On a scale of 1 to 10 (1 being low, 10 being high), how would you rate yourself in terms of greed?

2. We all enjoy nice things, but the issue is how high a priority we give to acquiring them. Why do you think greed is such an issue for many people, regardless of their vocational, social or economic standing?

3. Can you think of examples in the business world where you have seen unrestrained greed that resulted in damaging consequences? On the other hand, have you ever witnessed any positive, constructive benefits from greed? Explain your answer.

4. What solutions would you suggest to help someone who is struggling mightily with greed?

CHAPTER 22

PONDERING THE POSITIVES OF PATIENCE

In a world where many of us kneel at the altar of instant gratification, patience seems to be a virtue on the verge of extinction. We have fast-food restaurants because we don't want to wait for our food to be cooked. In our homes, microwave ovens present us with fully cooked meals within minutes, even seconds. When we cannot reach business associates at work, we dial their cell phone numbers or text them because we can't wait for them to respond to our voicemail messages.

Getting caught in heavy traffic frays our nerves and shortens our tempers because we're in such a hurry, impatient to get to wherever we're going. And these days, rarely do people remain with the same company for more than two or three years. Unlike people of decades past who labored long and steadily for an eventual promotion, many of us hop from job to job so we can advance careers on our terms – and at our own pace.

Yes, patience has become a lost art, but perhaps it is worth recovering. Just as Rome wasn't built in a single day, successful, fulfilling lives and careers can't be forged through haphazard, hasty, even impulsive actions. As difficult as it may seem in an age when attention spans rarely extend more than a few minutes (and often fade after mere seconds), there's something to be said about following the admonition found in the Bible that says, *"Be still before the Lord and wait patiently for Him"* (Psalm 37:7).

But we want to argue, "Be patient? Be still? Are you kidding? I have places to go and things to accomplish. So much to do – and so little time. I'm too impatient to practice patience!" If that seems similar to what you're thinking, it's understandable. But please – for just a few moments – consider some of the principles the book of Proverbs has to offer about this intriguing and perhaps counter-cultural topic:

Patience helps to accomplish your goals. Sometimes the "I must have it, and I must have it NOW!" attitude has the contrary effect of ruining opportunities to achieve desired goals. But by being patient and willing to take a long-term view, we can enlist the powers of persuasion to see important decisions change and also build support for desired outcomes. *"Through patience a ruler can be persuaded, and a gentle tongue can break a bone"* (Proverbs 25:15).

Patience quells unproductive anger. When things don't go the way we would want them to, it's easy to become angry and respond out of frustration. However, by remaining calm with emotions under control, we can avoid causing pointless damage to our relationships, our objectives, or our favorite causes. If we're patient, we may see circumstances change dramatically and experience outcomes far better than what we might have hoped for. *"Better a patient man than a warrior, a man who controls his temper than one who takes a city"* (Proverbs 16:32).

Patience puts out the fires of dispute. When someone comes to us in anger, it often triggers within us a "fight or flee" instinctive response. Trying to overcome anger with anger is like trying to put out a fire by pouring fuel on it. It is far better – and usually more effective – to respond to an unpleasant confrontation with patience, carefully listening to the problem being expressed and seeking its resolution in a calm, rational manner. Otherwise, a small skirmish could quickly escalate into full-scale combat. *"A hot-tempered man stirs up dissension, but a patient man calms a quarrel"* (Proverbs 15:18).

Patience instills needed discipline. The exercise of patience demands that we cultivate personal discipline to overcome impulsive behavior and unproductive emotional expression. It enables us to exhibit a sense of calm, even when we're fighting an inner urge that demands, "Do something, even if it's wrong!" *"Like a city whose walls are broken down is a man who lacks self-control"* (Proverbs 25:28).

Warning: Do not pray for patience, because the best, most expeditious way of acquiring patience is finding yourself forced to hang tough in situations where you have no other alternative than to be patient. Be careful what you pray for – you just might get it!

Putting It into Practice

1. Do you think people view you as a patient person? Why or why not?

2. What one factor or situation gives you the greatest difficulty in trying to exercise patience? Driving in traffic perhaps, or waiting for someone who is late for an appointment? Or maybe just listening attentively to another person, particularly one that's slow to get to the main point? What in your life challenges your patience the most – and why do you think this is so?

3. Have you ever experienced benefits from acting toward others with patience, or having someone demonstrate patience with you? Explain your answer.

4. What difference would it make, do you think, if you were to suddenly start being more patient in your interactions with others – at work, or at home – as well as being more patient in general when circumstances around you don't go as expected? How could you go about seeking to do that?

    Can – or should – trusting in God influence our ability to approach a situation with patience? If so, how?

CHAPTER 23

THE LEADERSHIP TRAIT BUSINESS SCHOOLS DON'T TEACH

What kinds of traits do we most typically look for in our leaders? Determination, dynamic personalities, the ability to get things done, magnetism that attracts and motivates others, self-confidence, vision and a strong sense of purpose are just some of the qualities we seek. You could probably list many more. Basically, we regard a good leader as someone who knows where he or she is going, knows how to get there, and inspires others to join in the journey.

But there's one trait you might not have considered: Humility. "Humble" is how you might expect to describe a mailroom clerk, or member of the custodial staff, but not the CEO or chairman of an organization. We want our leaders forceful and influential, not humble. However, in his book *Good To Great,* Jim Collins states that in a study of the 11 most consistently high-achieving companies in the United States, each of their leaders exhibited two specific qualities, one of which was great humility.

It's interesting that the Bible seems to offer a similar view on humility – and what might be regarded as its opposite characteristic, pride. Consider what the book of Proverbs has to say about both humility and pride:

Humility provides proper perspective. While success in business – and in life – is desirable, there's a danger of giving ourselves too much credit when things go well. Humility enables us to appreciate the circumstances that contributed to our success, as well as the people who helped to make it possible. *"When pride comes, then comes disgrace, but with humility comes wisdom"* (Proverbs 11:2).

Humility serves as a safeguard against disgrace. Pride that reflects satisfaction with one's accomplishments is normal and perfectly acceptable, but becoming unduly impressed with oneself, "thinking more highly of yourself than you ought," can lead to many problems – even profound embarrassment and utter defeat. Humility enables us to have the right attitude toward our successes, and receive recognition and rewards without becoming arrogant and overbearing. *"Before his downfall a man's heart is proud, but humility comes before honor"* (Proverbs 18:12).

Humility allows others the opportunity to honor what you have done. Most of us enjoy recognition for good work that we do, but people quickly tire of individuals who are boastful and shameless self-promoters. It is far more fulfilling to receive unsolicited praise than to draw attention to ourselves. *"Do not exalt yourself in the king's presence, and do not claim a place among great men; it is better for him to say to you, 'Come up here,' than for him to humiliate you before a nobleman"* (Proverbs 25:6-7).

Humility helps us to stay balanced. We all are born with unique skills, strengths and intelligence. We did nothing to earn or acquire these things; they were always "just there." What we did was develop what was already there. So rather than becoming annoyingly proud of traits we possessed from the start, humility enables us to acknowledge their source – God – and enjoy using them to the fullest of our capabilities. *"Humility and the fear of the Lord bring wealth and honor and life"* (Proverbs 22:4).

Humility reveals inner character. TV commercials used to urge us to "Look out for Number 1!" (our own interests), but a humble person is able to regard other people as equally important – or of greater importance – than himself. In the same way, our response to success – whether it causes us to become egotistical or simply thankful for the opportunities that came our way – shows the kind of person we truly are on the inside. *"The crucible is for silver and the furnace for gold, but a man is tested by the praise he receives"* (Proverbs 27:21, also see Proverbs 27:2).

PUTTING IT INTO PRACTICE

1. Do you enjoy being around people who are overly proud, boastful and arrogant about themselves and what they have achieved? Why or why not?

2. Be honest with yourself: Is pride an area where you struggle, in terms of your work and/or aspects of your personal life? If so, how has it shown to be a problem? If not, have you had to work to overcome it? Explain.

3. When you first read the word "humility" in this chapter, what came to your mind? Would you like to be known as a humble person? Why or why not?

4. How might humility be an asset in business situations you encounter every day? Are there situations in which you believe it could be a liability?

CHAPTER 24

THE INCREDIBLY HIGH COST OF ANGER

An earlier chapter in this book, "Anger: An Unnecessary and Dangerous Tool," originally was published as part of a weekly email workplace meditation series. Judging from responses it received from different parts of the world, it seemed evident that anger is a significant area of struggle for many of us regardless of the prevailing culture. Sometimes we can pinpoint the cause – a grievous personal loss that left us feeling helpless and resentful; frustration over experiences in the workplace or the home, or the pain of being treated wrongfully. In situations like that, a common reaction is to respond in anger. Sometimes, we can't identify a specific reason for this emotion, but feel angry and deeply agitated just the same.

We live in difficult, uncertain times. The world economy is unpredictable, sometimes seemingly conducting a dangerous flirtation with global calamity. Terrorism – unfathomable expressions of unprecedented hatred – has produced not only fear, but also intense anger and rage. Even normal workdays can spur us toward anger when we have to confront too many deadlines or address inordinate amounts of change. Years ago in a popular movie, one of the characters shouted, "I'm mad...and I'm not going to take it anymore!" It became the mantra of many people throughout the film. Have you ever felt that way?

While feeling angry is often understandable, the words and actions that arise from our anger can prove to be more damaging than the events that originally provoked our extreme emotions. Anger can result in both physical and emotional injury to other people. It can cause us to act irrationally. And anger can strongly influence how others perceive us.

Because anger is such a volatile emotion, and because this topic seems to have resonated with so many people, it might be helpful to consider additional wisdom about anger that we can glean from the pages of the Old Testament book of Proverbs:

Anger breeds carelessness. Have you ever lashed out to "get even" for something that someone else did or said to make you angry? Most of us have done this at one time or another; but an impulsive, careless, poorly considered response can make a bad situation even worse. *"A wise man fears the Lord and shuns evil, but a fool is hotheaded and reckless"* (Proverbs 14:16).

Anger invites conflict. When an angry person expresses his feelings, those present usually can't avoid responding in some manner. While some people may succeed in remaining calm, others are likely to react similarly in anger. *"As charcoal to embers and as wood to fire, so is a quarrelsome man for kindling strife"* (Proverbs 26:21). *"An angry man stirs up dissension, and a hot-tempered one commits many sins"* (Proverbs 29:22).

Anger can be controlled. In the aftermath of anger, after all the damage has been done, it's not unusual to hear someone say, "I'm sorry, but I couldn't help it." The truth is, they *could* "help it," but chose not to do so. Emotions – both positive and negative – can be controlled and expressed in appropriate ways. *"It is to a man's honor to avoid strife, but every fool is quick to quarrel"* (Proverbs 20:3).

Anger can be contagious. If you have a problem with anger – or even if you want to make certain you don't develop such a problem – avoid spending much time with angry people. Anger has a way of infecting other people, just as a drop of poison in a glass of water taints the entire drink. *"Do not make friends with a hot-tempered man, do not associate with one easily angered, or you may learn his ways and get yourself ensnared"* (Proverbs 22:24-25).

Anger is not a recommended character quality. What do you look for in a leader that you would be willing to follow – someone who is ruled by emotions, or someone who succeeds in keeping those emotions under control? Anger may motivate people into responding in a desired way, but in the long term it either creates fear or destroys trust. *"Better a patient man than a warrior, a man who controls his temper than one who takes a city"* (Proverbs 16:32). *"Mockers stir up a city, but wise men turn away anger"* (Proverbs 29:8).

PUTTING IT INTO PRACTICE

1. Be honest – do you sometimes struggle with anger? If so, can you identify reasons for anger being a recurring problem for you?

2. What about your working environment – do you see many other people who express anger in inappropriate ways? If so, how does that affect you and your attitudes during the course of the day?

3. Reread some of the verses from Proverbs in this chapter. What principles seem particularly important to you if you see the need to address this issue of anger – whether in your own life, or in the lives of people with whom you work or live?

4. Based on what you have read, what steps might be most effective in overcoming a persistent anger problem? How might you – or someone you know – start to implement these principles today?

CHAPTER 25

DILIGENCE DOES NOT HAVE TO EQUAL WORKAHOLISM!

One of the most perplexing challenges of everyday life is being able to achieve some semblance of balance in the things we do. It's not good to eat too much, but neither is it good to eat too little. We need regular periods of rest and renewal, but there's a time when rest must end, and activity and effort must resume.

The work we perform each day is another area where balance is needed – desperately. In an earlier chapter we expressed the view that good workers are diligent workers. When that particular piece was originally published as part of the weekly "Monday Manna" series, one reader wrote me and asked, "What is the difference between being diligent and being a workaholic?"

That's a very good question, an important issue for many of us in the business and professional world. Sometimes, working an exceptional number of hours may be necessary – especially when a deadline must be met and a project has to be completed on time. CPAs, for example, put in copious hours during tax season. However, when an excessively long workweek becomes the rule, rather than the exception, it's very possible the descent into workaholism has begun.

Work, like alcohol, can be addictive. Hard work, and achieving high results, can subtly shift from merely being a part of our lives to becoming the focus of our lives. I have no scientific data to document this view, but I believe more men than women are workaholics because work yields the tangible outcomes that many men seek, while spending time with their families may not produce the visible, quantifiable results they desire. Task-oriented goals are easier to track and measure than progress in relationships. (That doesn't make it right for men to concentrate on their work; it's just a reality that appears to be true for too many of them.)

So how can we be diligent in our work, without slipping into a workaholic lifestyle? After all, as we noted before, Proverbs 10:4 says, *"Lazy hands make a man poor, but diligent hands bring wealth,"* and Proverbs 21:5 tells us, *"The plans of the diligent lead to profit as surely as haste leads to poverty."*

All comes from God: The key is to realize that while we reap a reward from our labors, ultimately God provides for our daily needs. Who gives us health and strength? Where did we originally get the skills and talents we use each day at work? Even our interest in doing the kind of work that we do? We may have labored hard and with great determination to refine those abilities, but we all have innate traits that enable us to succeed in those things we enjoy doing. I would define "innate" to mean simply, the Lord put them there.

God provides; our work is the conduit. Years ago, I learned the best way to understand what God says in the Bible is to interpret it by what He says elsewhere in the Bible. For this reason, while the Scriptures exhort us to be diligent, they also advise us to avoid overworking: *"It is vain for you to rise up early, to retire late, to eat the bread of painful labors; for He gives to His beloved in his sleep"* (Psalm 127:2, NAS). We find a similar statement in Psalm 37:25: *"I was young and now I am old, yet I have never seen the righteous forsaken or their children begging bread."*

Based on these passages, it seems clear that a person who goes beyond diligence into workaholism is not doing it to meet daily needs. God promises to provide that for His children if they just do their part. We may overwork for a variety of reasons, such as:

- To pursue material lusts and desires.
- To build our egos with workplace accomplishments.

- To avoid painful issues we should be addressing and trying to resolve at home.
- To make work a "god," giving it a higher priority in our lives than our families, or even the true God.

Are you being a diligent worker – or a workaholic, addicted to your job? Only you can answer that, but the first step would be to ask yourself honestly, "Why am I working so hard?"

PUTTING IT INTO PRACTICE

1. Do you know someone who is a workaholic? What does someone like this look like, in terms of how they work and how they interact with people around them?

2. How would you distinguish being diligent – putting forth appropriate time and effort to complete a task or project – from being a workaholic?

   Are you convinced that "workaholism" is a less than desirable trait, or do you regard it actually as a quality to be admired – especially in the business and professional world?

3. Do you believe the statement that everything comes from God? Or do you subscribe to the belief that God may provide the basic resources, but from that point the responsibility lies fully on our shoulders – along the lines of, "God helps those that help themselves"?

4. Give your answer to the question raised in this chapter: *Are you being a diligent worker – or a workaholic, addicted to your job?* If you admit that you have a tendency toward a workaholic lifestyle, why are you working so hard?"

CHAPTER 26

THE BENEVOLENT – AND UNCOMMON – ART OF LISTENING

Has anyone – a coworker, a family member, even a teacher – ever asked you this question, "Are you listening?" There are many reasons (and convenient excuses) for not listening. We're tired. We're distracted by other concerns. It just may be that we're not interested in what someone is saying, so we have "tuned them out." I must admit to having been guilty of not listening more times than I can remember. On occasion, my wife has asked, "Are you listening to me?" and I've responded, "I heard you." But the truth was, even though I may have "heard" her, regretfully I wasn't listening.

There is a difference between hearing – the simple act of being conscious of the physical phenomenon of sound waves colliding with the eardrum – and listening. Unless you have an auditory disability, you can't avoid hearing. Listening, however, is another matter. That requires a conscious act of not only receiving sound waves, but also interpreting and applying meaning to the nerve impulses proceeding to the brain. To state it another way, hearing is an involuntary response to noise; listening is a voluntary activity. It may even be regarded as an act of kindness and respect.

For instance, a coworker complains or tells you about a circumstance that is causing personal pain. You may be busy with a project, but if you care about that person at all, you will choose not only to hear, but also to listen – at least for a brief time.

The same applies to situations at home, when a spouse or child wants to talk with you about something they consider important, even if you don't. Do you just "hear" what is said and, in effect, ignore them while you're concentrating on other matters? Or do you set those concerns aside long enough to genuinely listen, think about the information being presented, and respond appropriately?

Interestingly, a lot has been said and written about the importance of communication in the workplace – composing and reading memos, interoffice emails and reports, voicemail etiquette, actively participating in meetings, and making effective presentations. But rarely do we spend much time on what we might term "the benevolent art of listening." The book of Proverbs offers valuable insights:

Listening enables you to get to the real story. Frequently problems that arise at work are merely symptoms, the "tip of the iceberg." Solving them often requires getting to "the story behind the story," and there is no better way to do this than by listening attentively. *"The purposes of a man's heart are deep waters, but a man of understanding draws them out"* (Proverbs 20:5).

Listening helps to avoid calamity. Sometimes we feel there is nothing more important than what we have to say. But if we spend too much time talking and not enough time listening, we might not hear urgent warnings that are being offered. *"The wise in heart accept commands, but a chattering fool comes to ruin"* (Proverbs 10:8).

Listening prepares us for receiving much-needed correction. We all like commendation better than correction, but many times the most sensitive, caring thing someone can do is offer "constructive criticism" to show us how we can do better in the future. The key is striving to listen without becoming defensive, trusting that what is said is intended for our good. *"Like an earring of gold or an ornament of fine gold is a wise man's rebuke to a listening ear"* (Proverbs 25:12).

Listening enables us to respond appropriately. Often people share their hurts with us simply because they want to know someone cares about them, and also to receive assurance that there is still hope. If we take the time to listen, at the very least we demonstrate interest to the other person. By listening carefully, we may also be able to respond with just the right words for the moment. *"An anxious heart weighs a man down, but a kind word cheers him up"* (Proverbs 12:25).

So the next time someone says something to you, try to do more than just *hear* what is said. Also try to *listen* – what you receive through your ears may prove to be eye-opening!

PUTTING IT INTO PRACTICE

1. Think of a recent time when someone asked you, "Are you listening?" Or perhaps there's someone to whom you find it necessary to direct this question repeatedly. How often does this happen? Why do you think this is?

2. Do you agree with the distinction between hearing and listening? Why, in your opinion, is there a tendency to be so unskilled as listeners at the workplace and in the home?

3. What steps do you think could be helpful for someone who desires to learn how to become a better listener?

4. Do you concur with the statement that sincere listening is an act of kindness and respect? Why or why not?

CHAPTER 27

PUT THE ACCENT ON THE POSITIVE

W hen I was a boy growing up, I remember hearing a song that urged its listeners to "accentuate the positive, eliminate the negative." Frankly, in the troubled world of the 21st century, that seems like a tall order, a virtual impossibility. On a worldwide scale, we have ongoing war and violence in the Middle East, continuing repercussions from severe global disasters like earthquakes, hurricanes, horrific events like the tsunami in Asia, and economic uncertainties everywhere. In the business world, ever-intensifying worldwide competition and relentless change leave us feeling confused and perplexed. Hardly positive!

There's the story about the prominent executive who paused to reflect on the progress of his day, thinking, "Well, so far everything is going pretty well. No problems to this point…but in just a few minutes I'm going to get out of bed, and who knows what's going to happen after that!"

Have you ever felt that way? Sometimes it seems that if it were not for bad news, there would be no news at all. But years ago, Norman Vincent Peale wrote a best-selling book, *The Power of Positive Thinking*, that became extremely popular for years, not only in the United States but also in other parts of the world. He wasn't suggesting we ignore or deny things that go wrong. Instead, Peale pointed out our attitude toward life – and circumstances we encounter – can dramatically influence the likelihood of our success or failure.

From many centuries earlier, another collection of writings, taken from the amazing book of Proverbs, presents similar observations. In fact, it suggests a commitment to maintain a positive attitude not only affects our own success and satisfaction in life, but also can have a profound impact on those with whom we live and work. Consider a sampling of its comments about what happens when we endeavor to "accentuate the positive" God's way:

The healing power of a look, or an uplifting word. Do you have a member of your family, or know someone at work, who brings a smile to your face just by entering the room? People like this are a joy to be around, like a refreshing spring in an arid land. With just a little sincere effort, we can have a similar effect on others. *"A cheerful look brings joy to the heart, and good news gives health to the bones"* (Proverbs 15:30). *"Pleasant words are a honeycomb, sweet to the soul and healing to the bones"* (Proverbs 16:24).

Inward feelings shape outward appearance. In contrast, can you think of anyone who, simply by his or her usual demeanor, seems to drag a dark cloud into an otherwise sunny day? A sour attitude on our part can have that effect on others. At the same time, if we observe someone with a normally buoyant spirit who seems unusually downcast, this might be a signal for us to take a turn at offering encouragement, a caring, listening ear, or a helping hand. *"A happy heart makes the face cheerful, but heartache crushes the spirit"* (Proverbs 15:13).

A positive mindset contributes to physical health; negative thinking can result in physical decline. Author Norman Cousins recounted how he warded off the advances of chronic disease simply by laughing, aided in large measure by watching humorous films. He refused to dwell on the negative, despite the realities of his debilitating illness. Whether we are facing severe trials, or simply encountering difficult, short-term problems, a positive attitude can sustain our mental, physical, emotional and spiritual well-being. *"A cheerful heart is good medicine, but a crushed spirit dries up the bones"* (Proverbs 17:22). *"A man's spirit sustains him in sickness, but a crushed spirit who can bear?"* (Proverbs 18:14).

Offer hope, not platitudes. Keeping positive does not mean dismissing the burdensome realities of daily living. To deny, ignore or downplay the obvious, understandable pain another person is suffering serves in effect to withhold the compassion that is so desperately needed. Sometimes, rather than trying to offer simplistic comments to ease profound despair, our simple presence is sufficient to give someone hope. *"Like one who takes away a garment on a cold day, or like vinegar poured on soda, is one who sings songs to a heavy heart"* (Proverbs 25:20).

Putting It into Practice

1. Are you someone that likes to keep up-to-date on news developments, locally, nationally and globally? If so, do you find the daily bombardment of bad news discouraging? Do you find such reports affect your attitude for a prolonged period of time? Why or why not?

2. How do you regard your working environment – is it largely positive or negative? Explain, and offer an example. If your company's atmosphere tends toward the negative, can you think of ways you could exert a positive influence on those around you?

3. Thinking back to the question asked in this chapter, can you think of someone who usually brings a smile to the faces of people that he or she encounters? Why do you think this person has such a positive effect on others? Is this an innate "gift," or a quality many people could cultivate if they only made the effort to do so?

4. Do you believe that a person's mindset can have a significant influence on their physical health? Why or why not? What insights have you gained over the years on how to maintain a positive perspective on life?

CHAPTER 28

TRUTH...OR CONSEQUENCES?

For many years., one of the most popular TV game shows in America was "Truth Or Consequences." Basically, contestants were given a quiz and if their answers were correct, they would win a nice prize or reward. If they were wrong, they had to endure some type of penalty or "consequence." Obviously, everyone participating wanted to tell the truth. The alternative was not nearly as appealing.

In this game, the "truth" often amounted to a guess: For instance, trying to identify the correct price of a grocery item or an appliance, or answering a question properly. Contestants didn't always know the "truth."

However, in business, it's usually different. We *know* the truth: the quality or suitability of a product; the fair price for a sale item; whether we have been honest in submitting our expense accounts; or if we can meet a deadline according to the specified time frame. The question is whether we will *tell* the truth, or attempt to deceive by misrepresenting the facts.

Sometimes it seems the prevalent attitude in business is, "It does not matter what you do – even if it's wrong – as long as you don't get caught." This philosophy might work in the short-term, bringing about desired results without any readily apparent adverse impact. Over the long-term, however, the adage reminds us that eventually, "Your sins will find you out." Consider the wisdom about truth or consequences offered in the revered book of Proverbs:

Justice is inevitable. Admittedly, it sometimes seems as if unethical and immoral people "get away with murder." They do whatever they want to achieve their desires and goals, but no one seems to notice – or care. When we observe this, the temptation to do likewise can be very strong. At such times we must affirm to ourselves the value of a clear conscience, self-respect and an unsullied reputation. Sooner or later, the consequences of wrongdoing must be confronted. They can't be escaped. *"Be sure of this: The wicked will not go unpunished, but those who are righteous will go free"* (Proverbs 11:21).

The truth offers hope; the alternative is hopelessness. One of the great things about saying the truth – or doing the truth – is we don't have to try to remember our lies. And we can be assured that the outcome ultimately will be good. We might not make a much-needed sale, but we have maintained our integrity. And we don't have to wrestle with self-deceit. The danger and likelihood of untruthful speech and actions are that someday deceptions will be discovered, leaving us exposed, without a defense. It could cost us a prized business account, the trust of a valued associate, or perhaps our jobs – regardless of where we stand on the corporate ladder. Is the risk of such dire ramifications worth disregarding the truth? *"The desire of the righteous ends only in good, but the hope of the wicked only in wrath"* (Proverbs 11:23).

Rationalizing that a specific action is right does not make it right. If we want to do something badly enough that we know is wrong, we often can manage to devise many reasons to justify what we are doing. But whether we're cheating on our taxes, cheating on the time we spend at work, or cheating on our spouses, it's still wrong, no matter how much we pretend it's right or justifiable. Deep down, no matter how much we attempt to deny it, we realize when our actions are indefensible. Even more, God knows they are wrong and will accept no excuses. We all must answer to Him one day. *"There is a way that seems right to a man, but in the end it leads to death"* (Proverbs 14:12).

Truthfulness – and the lack of it – defines our credibility. There's sometimes a fine line between skillful negotiation and deliberate deception. People are willing to accept – or pay – a fair price for a service or commodity, realizing the need to make a profit and cover expenses. Again, misrepresenting the truth to "sweeten the deal" may succeed in the short term; but once people realize they have been misled, they're unlikely to put themselves in a position to be fooled or manipulated again. *"It's no good, it's no good!' says the buyer; then off he goes and boasts about his purchase"* (Proverbs 20:14).

PUTTING IT INTO PRACTICE

1. In your day-to-day business activities, how difficult is it to tell the truth? Are there times when it seems clearly to your advantage to distort the truth – or even to deliberately lie? Explain.

2. Do you believe those who misrepresent the truth eventually will face justice and suffer the consequences of their wrongdoing? Why or why not?

3. What are the benefits of being truthful in your speech and actions? What are the possible consequences of taking a stand for the truth?

4. Can you think of a time when you rationalized, convincing yourself that what you were doing was right – even though you knew in your heart it was wrong? What was the outcome of that particular situation? If you could redo that scenario, what would you do differently – if anything?

CHAPTER 29

GIVING: THE ENEMY OF POVERTY

At the end of each year, when the holidays are in full swing, we often hear conversations, public declarations, and even TV and radio commercials that extol the virtues of giving. Giving is central to the celebration of Christmas – after all, it is the time that people all around the world commemorate the birth of Jesus Christ, described in the Bible as God's greatest gift to mankind. Giving, of course, need not – and should not – be a practice restricted to special holidays.

Years ago I was fortunate to learn principles of giving from a variety of sources. I discovered, for example, the idea of stewardship. This means we're "stewards," or managers, not the owners of things entrusted to us, which include not only material possessions but also our talents and abilities, and our time. If you believe you truly "own" something – that it belongs exclusively to you – what will happen to it after you die? As much as we might like to deny the fact, we can't take it with us. To be a good steward, then, means to be willing to give from those things we alone have to offer.

Perhaps the most profound statement about giving I have ever heard came from a friend who for many years has led an organization to assist the poor in a very neglected area of his city. He told me, "The greatest poverty is the inability to give." One of the goals of his work has been to help the poor learn how to help themselves, thereby restoring to them the ability to give, along with the dignity and self-esteem that go with it.

This seems like a wonderful, far-sighted approach to addressing the needs of the poor. But it's also a principle we should all consider, even if we never expect to be classified among the destitute. Regardless of your level of affluence, according to that statement, if you fail to give from what you have, you are the poorer for it.

Why is the greatest poverty the inability to give? Why is it better than just keeping all you have and trying to acquire more? Proverbs offers helpful insights into this question:

When you give, you also receive. Do you remember in Charles Dickens' classic, *A Christmas Carol*, how Scrooge found joy only when he stopped hoarding his wealth? The former miser, after "seeing the light," became almost giddy in his generosity. *"One man gives freely, yet gains even more; another withholds unduly, but comes to poverty"* (Proverbs 11:24).

Giving does not diminish; it prospers. Like a saturated sponge that cannot absorb more until it's squeezed out, there seems to be a fundamental principle at work that insists we must first give from what we already have before we become capable to truly receive more. *"A generous man will prosper; he who refreshes others will himself be refreshed"* (Proverbs 11:25).

A generous spirit is readily recognized. Generosity is a quality that everyone finds attractive. Philanthropists are praised for their largesse, but even those who don't awaken each morning to great wealth are often commended for their eagerness to assist others in need. *"A gift opens the way for the giver and ushers him into the presence of the great"* (Proverbs 18:16).

Giving provides the joy of being able to help others. Being an instrument to assist in meeting the needs of others is a reward of its own. After observing the impact of their giving to enhance the lives of others, most people don't dwell on what they gave up; instead, they reflect on the privilege they've had of being conduits of aid for others. *"A generous man will himself be blessed, for he shares his food with the poor"* (Proverbs 22:9).

So whether you find yourself in the midst of the Christmas season, or at a totally different time of the year when we're not being constantly reminded of virtues of giving, make it a point to give – and give cheerfully. I'm confident you will discover that if you keep giving year-round, you'll be the better for it in many ways!

PUTTING IT INTO PRACTICE

1. When you hear messages about giving, whether through the media, a sermon or even a casual conversation, how do they make you feel?

2. How do you perceive the differences between an owner and a steward? In light of the distinctions between the two, would you conclude your own attitude toward what you possess requires any adjustment?

3. What do you think of the statement, "The greatest poverty is the inability to give"? Do you agree with it? Why or why not?

4. Would you like to be regarded as a generous person? If so, what changes in your approach to everyday life – if any – could be necessary? How might you go about making such changes?

CHAPTER 30

WORDS: TOOLS OF WONDER, TOOLS OF WOE

In an earlier chapter, we have talked about the power of the spoken word for both positive and negative effect. Since much of what we do in the business and professional world involves words – not only those we express verbally, but also those we use in contracts, mission statements, press releases, advertising, memos, emails, traditional letters, text messages on our cell phones, speaking to groups of all sizes – it merits looking a bit more at words and how we communicate.

Can you think of a time when someone made your day – or ruined it – by something he or she said to you (or didn't say)? For example, a friend told me about a boss he had who was quick to point out his failures, but refused to acknowledge his successes. As a result, the friend said he became discouraged. He felt he could never please his supervisor, no matter how hard he worked, and the encouragement he needed to maintain a high level of enthusiasm and dedication for his job never came.

Whether intended or not, what we say – as well as the things we choose not to say – communicate how we value others. It has been calculated that only seven percent of all communication is verbal; that is, actual words that are expressed audibly. The remaining 93 percent consists of nonverbal communication, which includes tone of voice, body language, volume, pace of speech, and eye contact. Nonverbal communication can also involve the words – and the ideas and feelings they represent – that go unexpressed. And that explains why my friend felt unappreciated, even though his boss never said anything specifically to that effect.

Words can be wonderful tools, tools that can inspire, uplift, motivate and challenge. Or they can have the opposite effect – deflating, disheartening and demeaning. Consider some of the principles about the proper use of the spoken word that we find in the ancient, yet timeless, book that is becoming so familiar to us, Proverbs:

Rightly chosen words carry great worth and weight. It's amazing to be with someone who consistently succeeds in finding the right words for a certain situation – as well as being able to do that yourself. Words chosen and utilized with care and discretion can dramatically transform a mood or perspective. *"The tongue of the righteous is choice silver, but the heart of the wicked is of little value. The lips of the righteous nourish many, but fools die for lack of judgment"* (Proverbs 10:20-21).

Sometimes silence is the best "speech." While words of encouragement are always welcome, sometimes it's better to say nothing than to express detrimental or even destructive thoughts. Just because an idea pops into our mind, this does not mean it must be verbalized. I fully agree with the famous statesman that said, "Better to keep silent and be thought a fool, than to speak and remove all doubt." *"A man who lacks judgment derides his neighbor, but a man of understanding holds his tongue"* (Proverbs 11:12).

Words used selectively can yield a sound investment. Many of us work diligently on our "to-do" lists, gaining fulfillment and satisfaction from a day of significant accomplishments. However, in the grand scheme of things, perhaps the best things we can do in any given day is to provide, for those with whom we work and live, lavish and genuine gifts of praise, encouragement, and sincere expressions of affection and appreciation. *"From the fruit of his lips a man is filled with good things as surely as the work of his hands rewards him"* (Proverbs 12:14). *"The wise in heart are called discerning, and pleasant words promote instruction"* (Proverbs 16:21).

Don't betray trust with careless words. It can be fascinating – and even give a sense of power – to know something that other people don't know, to possess some intriguing secret about someone that others would be delighted to hear. Of course, this "power" can only manifest itself when we provide our "audience" with this juicy "inside information" that only we can disseminate. In doing so, however, our trustworthiness with confidential information is diminished. And once trust is betrayed, it's difficult – even impossible – to recapture. This high cost, it would seem, is hardly worth the immediate gratification we experience. *"A gossip betrays a confidence, but a trustworthy man keeps a secret"* (Proverbs 11:13). *"A perverse man stirs up dissension, and a gossip separates close friends"* (Proverbs 16:28).

Putting It into Practice

1. Think of a time recently when an individual said something that dramatically altered – positively or negatively – your attitude toward the day and how it unfolded. What was said, and what effect did it have on you?

2. Consider the statistics that only seven percent of all communication is verbal (audibly expressed), while the remaining 93 percent is nonverbal. Have you found this to be true in your experience? Think of an example or two in which someone's actions and wordless manner – perhaps even your own – spoke more loudly than their words. Describe the message that was communicated and how it was received.

3. How effective do you think you are at choosing the right words for a given situation? If you believe you are successful at doing this most of the time, how did you learn or acquire this skill? If you feel a need for improvement in this area, how might you go about doing that?

4. Gossip is common – in the workplace, the neighborhood, and even in the home. Have you ever been victimized by malicious gossip? How did that feel, and what was its impact on you? Do you ever participate in gossip about other people? What about passing along confidential information simply to express "concern," or even to request prayers for an individual: Do you consider that to be "gossip? Why or why not?

CHAPTER 31

WHEN OPPORTUNITIES ABOUND, USE DISCERNMENT!

"When opportunity knocks, be sure to answer the door!" This seems like sound advice, without question, but it should come with a word of caution: Just because an opportunity presents itself, it's not necessarily the right opportunity for you.

Several years ago, for example, I was approached about becoming the managing editor of a high-quality magazine, one that had published a number of my articles. I was flattered by the possibility of taking a leadership role in the publication, but as I evaluated the situation it became apparent that for several reasons it would not be a good fit for me or my family. So I respectfully withdrew from consideration. In retrospect, it was wise decision because within a year the magazine was forced to fold, largely due to being undercapitalized.

There are other times when opportunities need to be considered in terms of our own limited capacity and personal resources. It's not that an opportunity is wrong or bad; it simply may require more time and energy than you can give to it, or it may prevent you from acting upon even more desirable opportunities.

The inspirational writer, Oswald Chambers, in his book, *My Utmost For His Highest,* writes, "The greatest enemy of the life of faith in God is not sin, but good choices which are not quite good enough. The good is always the enemy of the best" (May 25).

What a striking thought: Good being the *enemy* of the best! If this statement is true, how do we distinguish *good* opportunities that come our way from the very *best* opportunities? Particularly since what is merely good for one person, based on his or her interests, skills and gifts, would absolutely be the best pursuit for someone else? For instance, assuming a key leadership role in a volunteer organization may prove ideal for one individual, while the same role could cause great frustration for someone else with equal skill and talent, but whose passions and gifts lie elsewhere.

In addressing any area of uncertainty in life, including enticing opportunities, careful discernment is indispensable. Let's consider what the book of Proverbs has to say about being able to distinguish this difference between *good* and *best:*

Think through opportunities carefully before acting on them. When a new situation seems appealing, especially compared to what we presently are involved with, we can easily respond impulsively without thinking through all the possible ramifications. There is one ideal time to correct a bad decision: just before you make it. *"The wisdom of the prudent is to give thought to their ways, but the folly of fools is deception"* (Proverbs 14:8). *"A simple man believes anything, but a prudent man gives thought to his steps"* (Proverbs 14:15).

Consider opportunities rationally; don't let your ego get in the way. "You would be the perfect person for the job!" Has anyone said something like this to you? It's flattering to hear such effusive comments, but no one knows you as well as you know you. People generally mean well when they say such things. But sometimes they offer such encouragement to persuade, knowing a job needs to be done – and you seem to be the only one immediately available to do it. Don't be swayed by words that puff up your ego. *"The discerning heart seeks knowledge, but the mouth of fools feeds on folly"* (Proverbs 15:14).

Sometimes the best opportunity is the one you are already engaged in. Many of us like variety, and any job has moments when it seems hopelessly boring and routine. At such times we might start thinking about doing something new and fresh and different. After all, isn't variety supposed to be the spice of life? But if not carefully and cautiously evaluated, drastic changes can prove disappointing at best, disastrous at worst. *"A discerning man keeps wisdom in view, but a fool's eyes wander to the ends of the earth"* (Proverbs 17:24).

When opportunity knocks, you should answer the door – but that doesn't mean you are obligated to invite it to come in!

PUTTING IT INTO PRACTICE

1. How do you respond to the statement, "good is always the enemy of the best"? Can you recall when you agreed to take on a good opportunity – whether at work or in your personal life – only to realize that in the process you had turned away from an even better opportunity?

2. When it comes to discernment, how would you evaluate yourself? Do you tend to proceed with caution and great deliberation, or are you more inclined to act on impulse, according to your "gut feeling"? What are the advantages – and disadvantages – of both approaches?

3. Have you ever accepted an opportunity solely because someone convinced you that you were "the perfect person" for it, only to discover later that their assessment was wrong? Or can you think of someone else you know who made a wrong decision in large measure because someone appealed to his or her ego?

4. In another of his writings, Oswald Chambers states that, "a need does not constitute a call," meaning that just because something should be done, it doesn't mean you're the one that has to do it. How would you go about distinguishing a genuine need from a personal call to get involved in meeting the need?

CHAPTER 32

KINDNESS: THE BEST FORM OF REVENGE?

When was the last time that you felt someone had wronged you unjustly? It might have been five minutes ago, or yesterday, or last week. Most likely you don't have to think too hard or too long to remember a time when you were treated unfairly, regardless of whether the action was intentional or not. Even unintended wrongs can sting.

How did you react when that harmful act or inconsiderate gesture occurred, or some insensitive word was spoken? Did you respond directly, seeking to defend yourself or letting the person know how much you were offended? Or did you harbor the hurt privately, applying the balm of self-pity. Maybe you spent considerable time trying to determine how best to get back at the other person. "Don't get mad – get even!" is a motto some people like to apply in such situations.

And why not? If someone treats you wrongfully, isn't it appropriate to respond in like manner? "What goes around comes around" is another popular saying. But what if, instead of seeking to right the wrong by committing another wrong, you responded with kindness and compassion, simply overlooking the offense – or at least choosing to ignoring it?

You might be thinking, "Impossible! I need to let people know they can't push me around. If I don't stand up for myself, who will?" Who, indeed! Once again, the time-tested collection of wisdom we know as Proverbs presents a very different perspective – you might even consider it a radical, upside-down look – concerning this question of rights, wrongs, and revenge. Let's take a glance and consider just a few of the comments about this subject that we find in this ancient business manual:

Don't revel in another's misfortune. Two wrongs never make a right, an adage tells us. Being unjust to correct an injustice we have suffered only makes matters worse. *"Do not gloat when your enemy falls; when he stumbles, do not let your heart rejoice, for the Lord will see and disapprove and turn his wrath from him"* (Proverbs 24:17,18).

Don't distort your own case. In our desire to get even, there may be a temptation to embellish the facts to ensure our desired outcome. Again, this reduces us to the level of the one who wronged us in the first place. *"Do not testify against your neighbor without cause, or use your lips to deceive. Do not say, 'I'll do as he has done to me; I'll pay that man back for what he did'"* (Proverbs 24:28,29).

Condemn your foe with kindness. People who know they have treated us unfairly will expect us to respond in like manner. What would really catch them off guard – and perhaps even overwhelm them with remorse – would be to react in a way they clearly don't deserve. *"If your enemy is hungry, give him food to eat; if he is thirsty, give him water to drink. In doing this, you will heap burning coals on his head, and the Lord will reward you"* (Proverbs 25:21,22).

Trust God to make things right. The easiest thing to do when wronged is to act on our own behalf. For one thing, it feels good and relieves us of a lot of stress and bad feelings. But God promises to set things straight, if we don't get in the way by our own inappropriate actions. *"Do not say, 'I'll pay you back for this wrong!' Wait for the Lord, and he will deliver you"* (Proverbs 20:22).

PUTTING IT INTO PRACTICE

1. Think of a time when you felt you were treated unjustly – a time you are willing to discuss with others. What happened, and how did you feel? How did you respond?

2. Why does revenge seem so sweet? Can you think of a time when this initial "sweetness" later turned sour or bitter?

3. Why do you think God warns us in the Bible against taking our own revenge? Why would it direct us not to react in a manner that seems so fitting and justified when someone acts or speaks so unfairly against us?

4. Would you be willing to trust God to act on your behalf, rather than seeking your own vengeance? Why or why not?

CHAPTER 33

'HUMAN CAPITAL' IS CRITICAL TO BUSINESS SUCCESS

Enterpreneurs think in terms of innovative ideas and concepts. Visionary leaders talk about strategic planning and positioning. Financial controllers ponder bottom lines and cost effectiveness. Managers talk about productivity and efficiency. But when everything is considered, said and done, despite the differences in strategies and approaches these individuals utilize, there's one common, indispensable element required for any of their endeavors: People.

Over my years of directing newspapers, magazines and other printed communications, many of my most important decisions involved personnel. Finding the right people to do the right jobs can be at once exciting, challenging, fulfilling, difficult and frustrating. When you find a right fit – a person who is well-suited for and flourishes in a certain job – it's a joy for everyone to behold. But when you make a hiring error, or take a valued employee and place him or her in a new role, only to later discover they do not provide a good match, it can cause headaches that no popular pain remedy can relieve.

We sometimes refer to this as "human capital," the composite resources of the people that work for our companies: their experience, skills, talents, energy and initiative. We can have the best equipment and most advanced technology that money can buy, but without the right people doing the right work in the right places in the right way, our enterprises are doomed to great struggle, perhaps even failure. So how do we address this vitally important area of human capital?

Employment interviews, personal references, careful reviews of resumes, personality and proficiency assessments are very helpful, of course. We want to match education, expertise, abilities and interests to the responsibilities and expectations that a job will demand. But there are other equally significant factors worth considering as well. Here again the ancient book of Proverbs, nestled in the Bible's Old Testament, offers incredible insight:

Select people of proven character. Although the misdeeds of top executives receive the headlines, employees at any level can undermine the success, reputation and effectiveness of an organization. Rather than settling for favorable first impressions, it is wise to research potential employees carefully, gathering as much information as possible for determining whether they are the type of people we would want to become part of our corporate culture and represent our company and its values. *"Like an archer who wounds at random is he who hires a fool or any passer-by"* (Proverbs 26:10).

Seek people who possess not only knowledge, but also wisdom. It is one thing to know how to get a job done (knowledge); it is quite another to get a job done the right and ethical way (wisdom). Shortcuts – in traveling or in business – often result in unnecessary detours, even dead-ends. *"Do not set foot on the path of the wicked or walk in the way of evil men. Avoid it, do not travel on it; turn from it and go on your way"* (Proverbs 4:14-15). *"Stay away from a foolish man, for you will not find knowledge on his lips"* (Proverbs 14:7).

Strive to understand the needs of those who work with you and for you. Even if correct hiring decisions are made, the work isn't done. In fact, it has barely begun. Those who provide vital work for us still need nurture, attention and care. Often they require training and mentoring so they can carry out their responsibilities effectively and enthusiastically. With the right support and consideration, good employees can become great employees. Without it, potential – no matter how great – may never be fully realized. *"Be sure to know the condition of your flocks, give careful attention to your herds...the lambs will provide you with clothing, and the goats with the price of a field. You will have plenty of goats' milk to feed you and your family..."* (Proverbs 27:23-27).

PUTTING IT INTO PRACTICE

1. In your work, how much time and attention do you devote to "human capital" – the people who ultimately are responsible for accomplishing the work that must be done for your company's success?

2. What are your greatest challenges in finding and hiring the right people? Give an example.

3. Have you ever considered personal character among the necessary criteria for making important hiring decisions? Why or why not?

4. What are some things you can do to make sure that you "know the condition of your flocks"?

   Are you doing any of these things now? What changes do you think you should be making for the future?

CHAPTER 34

MOVING FORWARD WITH FAITHFULNESS

These are days when the most prized and sought-after virtues in workers include talent, intelligence, aggressiveness, enthusiasm and determination. And rightly so. Each of these qualities would seem to indicate someone of high productivity, skill and resourcefulness. "I wish all of my staff people shared those traits," many business leaders would agree.

Sometimes, however, important workplace values go unnoticed because they don't draw attention to themselves. One of these is *faithfulness,* which one dictionary defines as, "adhering strictly to the person, cause, or idea to which one is bound; dutiful and loyal; worthy of trust or credence; consistently reliable." While faithfulness is not typically a resume qualification that would separate one job candidate from the rest, it's a quality that can be readily recognized by its absence.

Faithfulness enables the worker to remain committed in the face of adversity and opposition. In a war, faithful soldiers stay in the battle; unfaithful soldiers flee or surrender. In business, faithful workers remain on the team despite economic reversals; unfaithful workers quickly update their resumes and seek new employment.

Granted, times and circumstances may dictate a need for change, but faithful people are those who can be counted on in a crisis, those individuals who serve as the firm foundation upon which successful enterprises are built and sustained. Are *you* a person who displays faithfulness?

To help you in answering this question honestly, consider the following insights from Proverbs:

Faithfulness is rare. We can quickly find people who want to be part of success, but not nearly as many that stay on to share in the struggle and risk potential failure. *"Many a man claims to have unfailing love, but a faithful man who can find?"* (Proverbs 20:6).

Faithfulness increases a leader's security. An effective leader would be wise to cultivate, recognize and reward faithful personnel, because they are the ones who remain and persevere during times of difficulty. *"Love and faithfulness keep a king safe; through love his throne is made secure"* (Proverbs 20:28).

Faithfulness is encouraging. The business adage, "It's lonely at the top," underscores the aloneness many leaders feel. They need faithful workers they can depend on, no matter what circumstances are presented. *"Like the coolness of snow at harvest time is a trustworthy messenger to those who send him; he refreshes the spirit of his masters"* (Proverbs 25:13).

Unfaithfulness betrays trust. Contrasted to faithful workers, unfaithful workers are of little or no value during the times when they are most needed. They prove as dependable as a leaky boat or a crutch made of rubber. *"Like a bad tooth or a lame foot is reliance on the unfaithful in times of trouble"* (Proverbs 25:19).

Faithfulness requires loyalty. The faithful person feels a strong sense of belonging to the leaders being served, the organization, or the cause. Abandoning that loyal commitment can prove painful for everyone involved. *"Like a bird that strays from its nest is a man who strays from his home"* (Proverbs 27:8).

Faithfulness involves patience. Sometimes the road to success is slow, bumpy, and marked with occasional and unanticipated detours. It's easy to become attracted to faster-moving endeavors that promise more excitement and immediate results. But in the end, the deliberate, even plodding path of faithfulness often proves the most rewarding and ful-filling. *"A faithful man will be richly blessed, but one eager to get rich will not go unpunished"* (Proverbs 28:20).

Putting It into Practice

1. On a scale of 1 to 10, 1 being low and 10 being high, how would you rate your faithfulness as a business or professional person? How about as a spouse? Or as a friend? Are your ratings consistent – or do you see distinct differences in your degree of faithfulness in different settings? Why do you think this is so?

2. How about the way others perceive you: Do you think those for whom you work would characterize you as being faithful? Why or why not?

3. If you're a leader, what do you think it means to demonstrate faithfulness to those who follow you? *Should* leaders that expect faithfulness also prove to be faithful to those who are following them? Explain your answer.

4. Think of a time when someone close to you – at work, in your home, or even a friend – was not faithful to you. How did it feel? How did you respond? Did this experience teach you anything about the value of faithfulness?

CHAPTER 35

FINDING THE RECIPE FOR RIGHT LIVING

We live in an age of moral relativism, a time when a prevailing mantra of society is, "There are no absolutes!" In many instances, the lines between right and wrong have become blurred, if not obliterated altogether. And yet, down deep, most of us would agree on what is right and wrong – at least in some areas.

For instance, none of us thinks it is good or right to have something stolen from us. We do not like being lied to, and a pattern of dishonesty can easily wreck relationships at work, at home, in friendships, and in community organizations. No one will justify an intoxicated driver who injures or kills other individuals as a result of reckless operation of a motor vehicle. We can agree that it is improper for a corporate executive to use privileged information for personal gain. It is wrong for an athlete to "shave points." The list could go on. We may not concur in every instance, but it seems we all have an innate sense of the right way to live – what the Bible refers to as "righteousness."

Looking at it from a positive angle, most of us would agree that assisting someone in need, whether due to health issues, financial difficulties or other problems, is a good and "right" thing to do. If we see someone being threatened with physical harm, it would be right to intervene on that person's behalf. Acts of kindness and compassion, along with words of affirmation and encouragement, are considered "right" and desirable.

Nonetheless, there are many areas of life where the issues of right and wrong are not nearly as clear-cut and conclusive. So how do we define what makes for "right living" when we shift from matters of black-and-white and move into the more debatable "gray" areas? While the book of Proverbs does not offer explicit guidelines for every specific circumstance, it does provide helpful guidelines and principles:

Right living reveals the correct path. When we see an individual living and working according to high moral and ethical standards, we become inspired. Often we desire to emulate such commendable behavior because we sense that's the way things should be done. *"The path of the righteous is like the first gleam of dawn, shining ever brighter till the full light of day. But the way of the wicked is like deep darkness; they do not know what makes them stumble"* (Proverbs 4:18-19).

Right living stays on course. People who seek to do what is right don't get sidetracked or choose alternative routes that appear to be more expedient. Their commitment to right living keeps them following a more narrow way, rather than taking roads that might seem more attractive and self-serving. *"Make level paths for your feet and take only ways that are firm. Do not swerve to the right or the left; keep your foot from evil"* (Proverbs 4:26-27).

Right living earns its own reward. There's not always a cause-and-effect relationship between doing what is right and seeing a positive return, but tangible rewards often do result. In addition, a guilt-free conscience, the satisfaction of a job well-done, and having the respect of one's peers are worthwhile goals and "rewards" in themselves. *"He who pursues righteousness and love finds life, prosperity and honor"* (Proverbs 21:21).

Right living is not based on feelings. A contemporary saying offers this suggestion: "If it feels good, do it." Emotions, however, are undependable, even deceptive as guides. We may feel angry enough to strike someone, but that would not make it right. And we may feel we are not being sufficiently compensated for our work, but that doesn't justify stealing from the company cash register. *"There is a way that seems right to a man, but in the end it leads to death"* (Proverbs 16:25).

Right living affects all of society. Our commitment to right living not only affects us personally, but also exerts great influence on the community around us, whether it's our home, our workplace, or the neighborhood in which we live. We can help to establish the standards by which we work and live, rather than having the standards created by someone else holding a different set of values. We can set the pace for determining and defining right and wrong. *"Righteousness exalts a nation, but sin is a disgrace to any people"* (Proverbs 14:34).

PUTTING IT INTO PRACTICE

1. How do you distinguish right from wrong in your life?

2. Do you find there are many "gray areas" in life, where the differences between what is right and what is wrong are not so easily distinguished? Discuss one or two examples that you think would fit this description.

3. The term "righteousness" sounds like a religious term, but at its essence, it simply means *right living*. Can you think of someone – a superior or peer at work, or someone in your family – whose life serves as a model of right living for you? How has this person influenced your own approach to life?

4. One of the Proverbs cited states "There is a way that seems right to a man, but in the end it leads to death"? Do you agree with this? If so, can you think of an example?

   If you subscribe to the philosophy, "If it feels good, do it," explain why you believe this is true.

CHAPTER 36

WHAT DO YOU REQUIRE IN A GOOD FRIEND?

What do you look for in a good friend? Someone with whom you can share some of your professional or recreational interests? Someone who is fun to be with, or has a good sense of humor? Someone who is usually available when needed? Or someone who always manages to lift your spirits?

Without question, valued friends can be any or all of the above, and we enjoy spending time with people like that. But most of these characteristics could just as easily be met by the family dog, cat or some other household pet. Doesn't it seem that true friendship should embody more than superficial behavior or an engaging personality?

I have been fortunate to have a number of genuine, devoted friends over the years, even though I never drew up a rigid set of "friendship requirements." But if you were to draft a job description for a good friend, what criteria would you include? Once again, a great resource to consult is the ancient book of Proverbs. See if the qualities presented below would fit among the traits you would desire in a good friend:

A good friend remains true during tough times. It's not difficult to find people who want to be around us when things are going well and they can benefit in some way from our prosperity. But what happens when a financial or vocational setback occurs, tragedy strikes, or you are faced with some other type of hardship that will not quickly disappear? *"A friend loves at all times, and a brother is born for adversity"* (Proverbs 17:17).

A good friend stays close and is unique. There is something special and distinctive about a truly good friend. We can accumulate acquaintances, people who enjoy some of the same things that we do, but how many of them would you entrust with your life, or with your most protected secrets? *"A man of many companions may come to ruin, but there is a friend who sticks closer than a brother"* (Proverbs 18:24).

A good friend demonstrates self-control. We all are influenced by the company we keep. If we're to achieve the lofty goals we set for ourselves, it helps to have friends who model self-discipline and inner character. *"Do not make friends with a hot-tempered man, do not associates with one easily angered, or you may learn his ways and get yourself ensnared"* (Proverbs 22:24-25). *"Do not join those who drink too much wine or gorge themselves on meat, for drunkards and gluttons become poor, and drowsiness clothes them in rags"* (Proverbs 23:20-21).

A good friend steers clear of evil. We wake up each morning to a world that tempts us to engage in unethical business practices, abusive forms of behavior, and all manner of immoral activities. Good friends have a positive impact on us through their personal conduct, and we should have a similar effect on them. *"Do not envy wicked men, do not desire their company; for their hearts plot violence, and their lips talk about making trouble"* (Proverbs 24:1-2).

A good friend offers sound advice. At times we all need to turn to someone for wisdom about making critical decisions. It's not a necessity to have a deep, personal relationship with someone when seeking sound advice, but trusted, caring friends can often provide the greatest insights into a perplexing situation – especially since they know us well. *"Perfume and incense bring joy to the heart, and the pleasantness of one's friend springs from his earnest counsel"* (Proverbs 27:9).

A good friend makes you a better person. There is something about good friends that can bring out the best in us. They challenge, motivate and inspire us. They pick us up when we're down, and show us ways that we can improve – professionally and personally. *"As iron sharpens iron, so one man sharpens another"* (Proverbs 27:17).

PUTTING IT INTO PRACTICE

1. Describe your best friend. What are the characteristics that make this person an important part of your life?

2. Often we select our friends based on roles they play in our lives – golfing buddy, lunch companion, financial advisor, business partner, etc. While those roles are legitimate and meaningful, do you agree that true friendships should be based on qualities deeper than just common interests? Why or why not?

3. Of the qualities or traits described in the verses from Proverbs, which seem(s) most important to you – and why?

4. Considering where you are in your own spiritual pilgrimage, would you regard God as a friend in any of the ways described in this chapter? Explain.

CHAPTER 37

'TIS THE SEASON TO BE PLANNING!

At the conclusion of each year, we pour our energies into planning in various forms. Planning for events surrounding holiday celebrations. Planning for gifts to exchange with friends and family members. Planning for the culmination of another calendar year in business, trying to finish as positively as possible. Planning last-minute adjustments for income and business taxes. Planning for end-of-year contributions to charitable causes. And planning for the coming year, seeking to devise strategies to ensure business will be better than it has been over the preceding year.

Planning is wise and necessary. The business or professional person who fails to carefully plan for the future is not likely to survive for long in today's fast-paced, highly competitive work environment. But as the adage reminds us, "The plans of mice and men often go astray." In developing plans of any sort, there are always factors we can't anticipate. The best we can do is to expect the unexpected, try to make allowances for it, and remain flexible. Because, whether we like it or not, circumstances often change at the most inconvenient moments.

In light of the many variables that influence the world of commerce today, formulating a sound business plan is like trying to move around an unfamiliar room in the dark – there are many obstacles that can trip us up. So how can we navigate the "unknowns" with any degree of success? An important first step would be to recognize the importance of including God in the planning process. Consider what the book of Proverbs has to say about this:

Plan with a higher goal in mind. If we plan to achieve only our own desires and objectives, we may fall far short of attaining the maximum good. God, who provides opportunities, along with bestowing our abilities, talents and resources, deserves and desires to be an integral part of the planning process. *"Commit to the Lord whatever you do, and your plans will succeed"* (Proverbs 16:3).

Plan with the awareness that your own knowledge and understanding are limited. Sometimes, even with the most diligent planning and preparation, circumstances can take sudden, unexpected twists and turns. We can attempt to resist these disconcerting developments, or we can deal with them proactively, trusting that God will use them, causing them to work for our benefit. *"Trust in the Lord with all your heart and lean not on your own understanding; in all your ways acknowledge him, and he will make your paths straight"* (Proverbs 3:5,6).

Plan with readiness to make course corrections if needed. No matter how thorough and meticulous our plans may be, we often find it necessary to make adjustments we could never have anticipated. While we may regard these as random occurrences, many times we later realize the changes came about as the result of divine guidance and intervention. *"In his heart a man plans his course, but the Lord determines his steps"* (Proverbs 16:9).

Plan with a willingness to serve God's greater purpose. We like to believe that we're in control, solely responsible for determining and achieving our own goals and objectives. However, in God's grand scheme of things, we serve as willing – or unwilling – instruments for carrying out His divine will and purposes. *"Many are the plans in a man's heart, but it is the Lord's purpose that prevails"* (Proverbs 19:21).

Plan with God, not against Him. In business we often see the value of making strong alliances, finding individuals and companies that provide synergy, helping us to accomplish our mission and goals through added resources and expertise. There can be no greater ally than God, whose knowledge, power and resources exceed anything we can imagine. To devise plans that we know run counter to His design and principles, then, is the height of foolishness. *"There is no wisdom, no insight, no plan that can succeed against the Lord""* (Proverbs 21:30).

PUTTING IT INTO PRACTICE

1. What are some of the primary areas where you are currently involved in planning? If you are reading this as the year is drawing to a close, or a new year is just getting started, what are your foremost plans and objectives?

2. Have you ever considered involving God in your planning process? If so, how have you done that – and how well do you think you're doing that now?

3. If you have never factored God's interests into your plans, does it seem strange or even troubling to consider doing so? Why or why not? If you were to engage God in your planning, how would you begin?

4. What difference would it make if your company resolved to acknowledge God's role in developing and carrying out a comprehensive business plan?

   Is this corporate perspective beyond the realm of possibility? Why or why not?

CHAPTER 38

CHECKUP TIME: HOW'S YOUR HEART?

Since heart disease is the leading killer in many societies, we read and hear a lot about how to properly care for our hearts. Exercise. Proper diet. Avoiding excesses of caffeine and alcohol. Not smoking. Maintaining the proper weight for our height and body structure. Getting regular health checkups to make sure blood pressure and other important physiological indicators are under control.

Heart problems can be particularly acute for hard-driving, success-oriented business and professional people who commit to doing whatever it takes to reach their goals – even if it means abusing their bodies and minds in the process. Some people take pride in thinking of themselves as "workaholics," and prefer to align with others who think and act the same way.

But there is another kind of "heart problem" that afflicts many of us. In this case, however, the "heart" pertains to our often-disguised objectives, the real motivations behind how we live, how we act toward others, even the things we say. Most of us enjoy being around people whose hearts are "right." They exhibit proven character and a commitment to integrity; they are individuals who are genuine and do not conceal hidden agendas. However, fierce competition and the lightning pace of today's high-tech business world seem to have turned people like that into an endangered species. As Proverbs 20:6 asks, *"...a faithful man who can find?"*

How is *your* heart? Are you a chameleon, a person who changes to fit the environment, quickly adjusting behavior and speech as necessary to accomplish a goal? If our motivation is focused on an intended end result, such as finalizing a deal or attaining a desired promotion, rather than the best interests of the people we're working with, it's easy to contract "heart trouble." Only by holding to values we believe in, letting them shape our behavior – rather than letting circumstances dictate our actions and values – can we succeed in maintaining healthy hearts in the workplace, as well as at home. Let's look at a few things the ancient book of Proverbs says about the heart:

The condition of our heart is a good indicator of who we really are. Have you ever looked closely in a mirror and discovered a blemish that you didn't realize was there? The blemish can't be blamed on the mirror – it merely reveals the truth. The heart functions the same way in revealing our inner selves. *"As water reflects a face, so a man's heart reflects the man"* (Proverbs 27:19).

A healthy heart attracts good company. We can build strong, mutually beneficial relationships when people know for certain they can trust and rely on us, regardless of the circumstances. *"He who loves a pure heart and whose speech is gracious will have the king for his friend"* (Proverbs 22:11).

A diseased, deceitful heart eventually will be discovered. We may succeed in deceiving people for a while, but inevitably our duplicity will be revealed. *"A malicious man disguises himself with his lips, but in his heart harbors deceit. Though his speech is charming, do not believe him, for seven abominations fill his heart. His malice may be concealed by deception, but his wickedness will be exposed in the assembly"* (Proverbs 26:24-26).

One of the best ways of ensuring a good heart is to stay close to its Creator. If I want my car to continue operating properly, I would be wise to follow the guidelines given in the owner's manual and take the vehicle to a repair shop for scheduled checkups. In striving to have a good heart, professionally and personally, we would do well to follow a similar practice by observing the instructions God provides in the Scriptures. *"Blessed is the man who always fears the Lord, but he who hardens his heart falls into trouble"* (Proverbs 28:14).

Putting It into Practice

1. Have you had a physical exam recently? Was it a regular checkup, or was it necessary because of a specific problem you were experiencing? What was the outcome of the checkup? How's your heart doing?

2. When was the last time – if ever – that you had a "checkup" for the other kind of heart that this chapter speaks of? If someone could look into you and see this heart – your motivations – what do you think they might find?

3. Can you think of a specific situation in which your attempt at deceiving someone or manipulating circumstances to your advantage was discovered? How did it feel to be "found out"?

4. The truth is, not one of us can boast having a pure heart at all times. Often pride, selfishness and other motives rise up to tempt us to manage or manipulate circumstances for our advantage. What steps might you take to make sure your spiritual "heart" undergoes a regular checkup? Could some form of personal accountability be helpful?

CHAPTER 39

WHAT IS *REAL* LIVING?

Not long ago I was meeting with a group of men during lunch and our discussion centered around the question, "What is real living?" Interestingly, answers were not as easy to find as we might have thought, and when we did propose answers, the responses were remarkably diverse.

One man suggested that real living is "enjoying the best things in life." Another commented, "having fun and avoiding as much drudgery as possible." Eventually, the discussion took a more serious turn as people admitted that while material things and enjoyable activities can enhance life, "real living" must involve intangibles that can't be packed into a box or scheduled on a calendar.

Many centuries ago, Jesus was talking with His followers about real living. He stated, "I have come that they may have life, and have it to the full (or, *abundantly*)" (John 10:10). But what does it mean to have life "to the full" or "abundantly"?

To find some meaningful answers, in this chapter we will consult the book of Proverbs, along with a few other insightful passages from the Bible:

Real living involves purpose. An important element to the success of any enterprise is having a definitive, clearly articulated mission statement – a thoughtful expression of its purpose, its reason for existence. As individuals, we also need a "mission statement" of sorts. It's important to have an understanding of why we exist. Without a sense of purpose, we can easily engage in empty pursuits, activities that seem appealing but ultimately have no positive or enduring results. In 2 Timothy 3:10, the apostle Paul wrote, *"You, however, know all about my teaching, my way of life, my purpose, faith, patience, love, endurance...."* He had a clear idea of where he was going and how to get there.

Real living involves working. Work is not some "necessary evil," but one of the ways we can utilize our personal skills, experience and innate gifts both for personal fulfillment and for the benefit of others. Contrary what some people believe, living to the full does not mean avoidance of work. Work is an expression of who we are and what we were designed to be. The key is to understand that "design" and determine how best to put it into practice. *"One who is slack in his work is brother to one who destroys"* (Proverbs 18:9).

Real living involves loving. We live in a narcissistic world in which so many people around us typically ask, "What's in it for me?" However, one of the most profound and compelling human emotions is love, which requires reversing our typically inward focus and turning it outward. There is romantic and sexual love, but also love for family, friends, one's country, and even love for a noble cause or mission. When love is expressed through selfless action, real living increases in both depth and breadth. *"Greater love has no one than this, that he lay down his life for his friends"* (John 15:13). *"Love and faithfulness keep a king safe; through love his throne is made secure"* (Proverbs 20:28).

Real living involves giving. A selfish view of life focuses on what one will receive, but as Jesus said, *"... 'It is more blessed to give than to receive'"* (Acts 20:35). It is a curious truth that when we give – whether from our material possessions, our time and energy, a listening ear or even a kind word – we also receive. Receiving is only a one-directional act, but when we engage in the process of giving we also receive, engaging in genuinely two-way, two-directional behavior. One of the greatest joys in life comes from knowing that something we give can enhance and improve the lives of other people. *"He who despises his neighbor sins, but blessed is he who is kind to the needy"* (Proverbs 14:21).

Are you interested in *really* living? Following and applying the principles above would serve as an excellent start in that direction. Live with purpose. Live through your work. Live with love. Live by giving.

Putting It into Practice

1. Before reading this chapter, if someone had asked you the question, "What is real living?" how do you think you would have responded?

2. Do you agree with the contention that "real living" involves more than the acquisition of desired material things or engaging in pleasant, appealing activities? Why or why not?

3. Would you say that you have a defined purpose or clear sense of mission for your life? If you do, what is it? If not, do you think it could be worthwhile to take the necessary time to determine what your personal purpose or mission should be? Explain.

4. Do any of the principles cited for real living seem particularly significant for you? If so, which one(s)?

   Can you think of any other principles that also might be helpful for someone interested in discovering what "real living" is all about?

CHAPTER 40

WHAT KIND OF LEGACY WILL YOU LEAVE BEHIND?

When your time on earth has ended, how do you think you will be remembered? Let me ask the question a little differently: How would you *like* to be remembered?

The distinction between these two questions is very important. For instance, I might *desire* to be remembered as a warm, caring, generous person. However, if I am cold, uncaring and not generous toward others, that's the way people will remember me, not the way I *want* to be remembered.

If you're like me, you can think of at least several people who have had a positive impact on your life. The people who come to my mind are those that served as strong examples of how to live and how to give of themselves. They took a genuine, unselfish interest in me and inspired me to develop my gifts and abilities more fully. Then there are people I have never met – writers, artists, public servants and leaders – who demonstrated, through words and deeds, what it means to strive to live in the image of God.

When we speak in terms of how people will remember us after we pass from this life, we're thinking in terms of the *legacy* we will leave behind. Like a stone thrown into a lake that disappears and leaves only ripples behind, what will be the nature of the "ripples" we leave behind when our earthly lives have come to an end?

This is a question of profound importance. When I originally wrote this, I was already in my mid-50's and realized that in a practical sense, more of my earthly life is behind me than lies ahead of me. That's even more the case today. The reality is, not one of us knows for certain how much life we have left. So, based on what you have done thus far – and what you expect to accomplish in the time that remains – what kind of legacy will *you* leave behind?

Once again, the book of Proverbs offers great insight. Basically it tells us that a key to leaving a meaningful, positive legacy is what we might call "right living," as we have considered in a previous chapter. Proverbs uses words like "righteous," which means to live in the right way. Consider the following:

A life poorly spent is soon forgotten. The legendary industry leader and innovator Howard Hughes was one of the world's richest men, but by the time he died, he had deteriorated into an eccentric, paranoid recluse. He could have done so much good with his wealth, making a difference in many lives, but instead, his riches controlled and corrupted him. *"The memory of the righteous will be a blessing, but the name of the wicked will rot"* (Proverbs 10:7).

A life well-spent will bear fruit for a long time, making it an excellent investment. Some of the richest people in life are those who don't make huge financial investments, but who give freely of what they have – their time, talent and personal resources – to benefit others. Their reward can't be measured in terms of money or material possessions, but rather by the enhanced lives of others. *"The fruit of the righteous is a tree of life, and he who wins souls is wise"* (Proverbs 11:30).

Lives guided by evil intent do not leave lasting legacies. When we see people prospering at the expense of others, we can be assured their "success" will quickly fade, like the light of a candle once the flame is blown out. *"The light of the righteous shines brightly, but the lamp of the wicked is snuffed out"* (Proverbs 13:9). *"Do not fret because of evil men or be envious* *of the wicked, for the evil man has no future hope, and the lamp of the wicked is snuffed out"* (Proverbs 24:19,20).

To establish a worthwhile legacy, spend your life on things that will last. "You can't take it with you," the adage reminds us. When our lives come to an end, it will no longer matter how much money we had in the bank, how many cars we owned, how big our houses were, or whether we could afford to eat in expensive restaurants. All that matters – our legacy – will be the impact we had on the lives of people God brought into our sphere of influence. *"...for riches do not endure forever, and a crown is not secure for all generations"* (Proverbs 27:24).

PUTTING IT INTO PRACTICE

1. If your life were to come to an abrupt end one hour from now, what kind of legacy would you be leaving behind? To put it another way, how do you think you would be remembered?

   Is this the kind of legacy that you would *want* to leave behind? Why or why not?

2. If the legacy you would *expect* to leave behind does not match the legacy you would *want* to remain after you are gone, what changes do you think might be necessary?

   Which of these changes do you think you could start making immediately?

3. Can you think of any well-known people, perhaps those who commanded prominent headlines during their lives, who have become virtually forgotten following their death? Since their lives attracted so much attention, why do you think memories of them have faded so quickly?

4. Consider the verses from Proverbs that have been included in this chapter. What do they say to you personally? Until now, have you ever seriously taken the time to consider what kind of legacy you are establishing over the course of your life?

Perspectives
Beyond
Proverbs

CHAPTER 41

HOW TO HAVE A JOB YOU LOVE

S ome of us are fortunate to have jobs we truly enjoy. But according to studies, the vast majority of men and women in the business and professional world dislike or even hate their jobs; at best, they tolerate what they have to do every day to earn a living. Are you among them?

Would you like to be able to say with sincerity, "I love my job!"? What do you think it would be like to begin each day with eager anticipation, looking forward to the opportunities and challenges you will encounter at your workplace – rather than approaching them with dread and anxiety? "Well, I would have to change jobs!" many people would agree. Perhaps, but recently I heard an intriguing story that seemed to indicate a new place to work might not necessarily be required for finding a job you love.

At a cancer support group meeting I attended (my wife is a cancer survivor), a woman was telling about an inspiring person she had met while going for her treatments – a valet parking attendant. "This woman was amazing," she said. "She truly loved her job – and she loved each of us, patients at the hospital where she worked, as we would arrive each day for our appointments. She never failed to have a big smile and an uplifting word of encouragement for each of us.

"She made the greatest impression on me," the speaker at the meeting observed. "She would be out there every day, even in scorching heat and freezing cold, focused on greeting each patient and helping to make their day a little bit brighter."

Being an administrator for a non-profit organization, the woman telling this story thought to herself, "This is the kind of person we need to hire as our new receptionist." In fact, she offered the job to the parking attendant. The woman, with her customary smile, politely declined. She explained she could never leave her job – not that it paid particularly well, but because in a real sense it had become her "dream job." She looked forward to each day and the opportunities to offer a kind word, give someone a needed smile, or shine a ray of hope for someone desperately needing it. In a word, she saw her job as *ministry.*

What if we each took that same attitude, viewing our work as a ministry – an opportunity to serve and be of help to others – rather than simply a source of a paycheck or a way to fill time between weekends? But how can we possibly do this, especially if circumstances are far from ideal? Consider this advice from the Bible:

Focus on the positive. Undoubtedly, aspects of the parking attendant's work weren't perfect; surely there were things she would change if she could. But instead, she was concentrating on others. *"Finally, brothers, whatever is true, whatever is noble, whatever is right, whatever is pure, whatever is lovely, whatever is admirable – if anything is excellent or praiseworthy – think about such things"* (Philippians 4:8).

Remember whom you ultimately serve. In our jobs we must envision doing our part in something much bigger than ourselves. Centuries ago, someone observed a brick mason and asked if he ever grew tired of his work. "No," he replied, "because I'm building a cathedral." He saw beyond bricks and mortar; he envisioned himself engaged in an important, life-changing enterprise. *"Slaves, obey your earthly masters in everything.... Whatever you do, work at it with all your heart, as working for the Lord.... It is the Lord Christ you are serving "* (Colossians 3:22-24).

PUTTING IT INTO PRACTICE

1. No question, every job has aspects of it that are less than ideal. Yet some people seem to truly love their jobs, regardless of negative circumstances. Do you know someone like that? What is it about such people that enables them to look to each workday with eagerness and anticipation?

2. What's the predominant attitude you have toward your own work? Whether you regard it very positively – or negatively, what is it about the job that you think makes you feel that way?

3. In your mind, what does it mean to view a job as "ministry"? Do you think it would change your approach to your own job if you viewed it in this way?

4. Do you think either of the Bible passages would be helpful for adopting a more positive, motivating attitude toward your work? Explain your answer.

CHAPTER 42

WHOSE JOB IS MOST IMPORTANT?

I f someone asked you whose job is most important where you work, what would you say?

Would it be the CEO, chairman, or owner of the company? When evaluating jobs in terms of importance, we typically look at top position on the corporate ladder or organizational chart, such as the top executive. Other factors can include compensation and productivity level. If a person is paid a lot, he or she must be worth it, right? And the top salesperson in any business would rank high. Without someone generating sales to keep business coming in and products or services going out, the company would eventually have to close its doors.

But there's another way of assessing one's importance in the workplace. I was reminded of this during a conversation with a manager at a company I've been working with over the last several months. The plant, which manufactures products outsourced by Fortune 500 companies, depends upon the consistent, quality work of many key people at various steps in the manufacturing process

For instance, the procurement department must ensure that materials are available when needed to make a specific product. If the materials are not on hand, the production line can't run. So people in procurement are very important. The manufacturing department also ranks high in importance – how can you sell a product you haven't made? The maintenance department is poised to make critical repairs to machinery when necessary, so its work is of paramount importance as well.

Then there's the accounting department, which sends invoices, collects payments and pays suppliers. People in the payroll and human resources departments play crucial roles in terms of ensuring employees are paid promptly and receive benefits to which they're entitled, hiring new staff members when needed, and handling the process when employees retire or must be terminated.

So at that company – as with all organizations where we work – the most important job, or most important person, depends upon what must be done at any particular moment. Even the custodial staff can be considered most important when it comes to maintaining hygienic and well-supplied restrooms, disposing of trash, and keeping floors vacuumed and offices cleaned. This helps us to realize two important principles:

Don't overestimate or underestimate your own importance. Even if you rank near the top of your company's organizational chart, your effectiveness and productivity are integrally related to the work performed by others. And if you hold a lower-level role in your organization, you're still important. Even the best, most experienced speaker must rely on someone else to make sure the microphone is ready and the sound system is functioning properly. *"Do not think of yourself more highly than you ought, but rather think of yourself with sober judgment, in accordance with the faith God has distributed to each of you"* (Romans 12:3).

Do not underestimate the importance of others. There can be a temptation to disregard individuals of lower standing within a company, but every job is crucial to its success. Each person should be appreciated and affirmed for what they do and their role in the overall corporate effort. *"Do nothing out of selfish ambition or vain conceit, but in humility, consider others better than yourselves"* (Philippians 2:3).

PUTTING IT INTO PRACTICE

1. When you first read the question, "Whose job is most important where you work?" what was your answer? Why?

2. How would you assess the importance of your own job?

3. What are your thoughts about the idea that every job – and every person performing that job – is important, and depending on the specific need of the moment, that particular job could actually be the most important within the organization?

4. Has this discussion caused you to reconsider how you regard the various jobs undertaken at your company – and the people that perform them? Is your response to "Whose job is most important where you work?" any different now that you've read this chapter? Explain your answer.

CHAPTER 43

LEARNING FROM THE MISTAKES OF OTHERS

"Why do you want to be mentored?" That was the question I asked the young man sitting across the table from me at a local restaurant. A mutual friend had suggested to Todd that he meet with me since he had expressed interest in having someone mentor him for both his professional and personal life.

His answer surprised me: "I want to learn from your mistakes." I smiled, thinking here was a man in his late 20s that already had the wisdom to recognize that you don't have to learn exclusively from your own errors and poor decisions. You can learn from people that have already traveled along the path you're following – and can benefit from what they have learned through trial and error.

As it turned out, he and I did not begin a one-to-one mentoring relationship because he already was meeting with several other men in various mentor-like capacities. With many younger men lacking even a single man to meet with, I concluded Todd already had enough help. But his comment caused me to reflect on the many times I've done the same thing – learned from the mistakes others have shared with me, along with their successes.

I wouldn't have the passion I have today for helping others learn how to effectively integrate their faith in the workplace if it hadn't been for others that showed me it could be done. And they honestly told me about times when they had failed, such as times they yielded to the temptation to cut corners to achieve goals, even though they knew it would be a breach of their personal integrity.

It was through failures like these, however, that they learned the importance of setting boundaries, of affirming their commitments to excellence and honesty before they came to a moment of decision. Difficult decisions become easier, they taught me, when they're made well in advance of the crisis.

Men like these also taught me about their trials, failures and successes in areas such as marriage, parenting, handling finances, dealing with anger and other troublesome emotions, and sexual temptation. I, too, have been privileged to learn from the mistakes of others.

The Bible offers many character studies of men that strived to follow and serve God, yet sometimes stumbled along the way. I have found these stories very encouraging, not only by learning specific details of their failures, but also realizing God does not demand perfection, only a sincere desire to follow Him, along with a willingness to repent in times of failure. The 10th chapter of 1 Corinthians offers great insight from just two verses:

Recognize other people's failures and take them to heart. There's a saying that if we fail to learn from history, we are doomed to repeat it. Colleagues and friends can only be bad influences when we allow ourselves to repeat their wrong actions. *"All these things happened to them as examples, and they were written for our admonition"* (1 Corinthians 10:11).

Don't overestimate your own strength and resolve. One of the benefits of learning from the mistakes of others is realizing we could make the same errors. If we're wise, we will take preventative steps to avoid a repeat of those failures. As another saying tells us, an ounce of prevention is worth a pound of cure. *"So, if you think you are standing firm, be careful that you do not fall!"* (1 Corinthians 10:12).

PUTTING IT INTO PRACTICE

1. Have you ever taken the opportunity to learn from someone else's mistakes? If so, give an example of when you did this – and what you learned.

2. Have you ever given anyone a similar opportunity to learn from *your* mistakes? Explain your answer.

3. Can you think about a time when you should have learned from hearing about or observing another person's mistakes, but instead proceeded to repeat the error? What were the consequences for you?

4. Reading the Bible we can find numerous case studies of people who made serious mistakes, yet were forgiven and restored in their relationship with God. Do any specific examples come to your mind? Knowing that individuals like this failed, yet were not abandoned by God, does this encourage you in considering your own actions? Why or why not?

CHAPTER 44

ISSUING A DECLARATION OF DEPENDENCE

Have you noticed how children can't wait to achieve independence? Infants, of course, are fully dependent for being fed, bathed, clothed, even being transported from place to place. But after children reach a certain age, often as young as two years old, they instinctively start asserting their "declaration of independence."

For instance, you try to help a child putting on her shoes, and she dismisses your efforts: "I do it!" the independent little one declares. Perhaps you offer to help the little boy finish the last bite of food off his plate. "No, I do it!" he responds emphatically. Parents want their children to become independent eventually, just not at the ages of two or three.

This impulse toward self-reliance and self-sufficiency remains strong throughout our lives. Many people dream of becoming "financially independent," reaching a point when a regular paycheck is no longer their compelling motive for working. Others yearn to fill the description offered by the hero of "Invictus," written by William Ernest Henley. In this brief poem, first published in 1888, the central figure declares, "I am the master of my fate: I am the captain of my soul."

It seems commendable to want to be master of your own fate, to take full responsibility for the outcomes of your own actions and decisions. However, complete independence has a downside.

In the Old Testament of the Bible, we read about Uzziah, who for 52 years served as king of Judah. We are told, *"He did right in the eyes of the*

Lord.... As long as he sought the Lord, God gave him success" (2 Chronicles 26:4-5). For much of his life, Uzziah openly acknowledged dependence on God for his prosperity.

However, a time came late in his royal reign when success apparently went to Uzziah's head. Even when confronted about his rebellion, he refused to accept accountability and correction. *"...His fame spread far and wide, for he was greatly helped until he became powerful. But after Uzziah became powerful, his pride led to his downfall. He was unfaithful to the Lord his God..."* (2 Chronicles 26:16-21). Uzziah had become self-sufficient; he felt he needed no one, not even God.

This king lived thousands of years ago, but human nature hasn't changed much since then. Many of us, early in our business or professional careers, realize success is beyond our grasp. We turn to others – even God – for aid in getting established, especially when job responsibilities and pressures seem overwhelming. Once success is attained, however, we can easily forget and lose that sense of dependence. "I have pulled myself up by my own bootstraps," we might conclude, basking in self-adulation.

As King Uzziah learned, this attitude usually leads to disaster. Failing to recognize help received in climbing the "ladder of success," as well as support for continued success, can foster false pride – and expose our vulnerabilities to competitors and opposition. The Bible tells how to avoid such calamity:

Recognize God as the source of wisdom and success. There are many avenues we can pursue in our quest for building a successful life and career, but the enduring teachings of the Bible have guided people for thousands of years – and they haven't gone out of date. *"Do not let this Book of the Law depart from your mouth; meditate on it day and night, so that you may be careful to do everything written in it. Then you will be prosperous and successful"* (Joshua 1:8).

Welcome correction and reproof. Willingness to consider and respond to correction reflects wisdom and the humility to have someone show us where our lives might have gotten off track. *"He who ignores discipline comes to poverty and shame, but whoever heeds correction is honored"* (Proverbs 13:18).

PUTTING IT INTO PRACTICE

1. How have you seen young children display the natural impulse for independence?

2. Do you agree that there's a negative aspect to asserting our independence? Why or why not?

3. What's your reaction to the brief account of King Uzziah? Read the remainder of the 26th chapter of 2 Chronicles and consider your reaction to how the king demonstrated belief in his self-sufficiency and the consequences he suffered as a result.

4. Would you say that you're in any danger of becoming too self-reliant? If so, what steps might you take to maintain a healthy balance between independence and dependence, whether that means reliance on God, colleagues where you work, or even members of your family?

CHAPTER 45

THE BEST THINGS ALWAYS TAKE TIME

It used to be said that "a watched pot never boils," but with the advances in technology, a more current version of this saying might be, "a watched microwave never beeps." It seems that whether in business, family matters, cooking a meal, or simply going through the process of experiencing everyday life, we're in a hurry. We don't want to wait for anything. "I want it – and I want it NOW!"

In reality, however, the best, highly cherished things in life almost always require time – and lots of it. Prospective physicians attend college, then spend more years going to medical school and receiving training in their chosen specialties. To earn a prized MBA, business and professional people must invest much more time and expense beyond their undergraduate years in college.

We all have been confronted with "get rich quick" schemes at one time or another, but the most certain way to attain financial security is through careful and judicious spending, wise investments and well-thought-out plans for the future. As the Bible states, *"Dishonest money dwindles away, but he who gathers money little by little makes it grow"* (Proverbs 13:11). It also observes, *"Steady plodding brings prosperity; hasty speculation brings poverty"* (Proverbs 21:5).

Some of the most priceless qualities of life also are products of time. For instance, parents of teenagers just starting to drive feel anxious, usually not because they lack trust in their children, but because they know *experience* cannot be taught – it can only be gained through practice. Professionally the same is generally true, whether you're an airline pilot, computer programmer, or CEO.

The same applies to *wisdom.* Intelligence and skill can be gained through classroom study, workshops and specialized training. But wisdom – the effective application of knowledge through understanding and insight – must be acquired over extended periods of time. If it were possible to store wisdom in a package, it would find an unlimited market and generate an instant fortune. However, wisdom can't be bottled or manufactured. It must be developed over the process of daily living, learning from success and failure.

So how can we successfully "bide our time" as our greatest hopes, aspirations and goals seem to remain just beyond our reach? The Bible offers some sound suggestions:

Resist questionable shortcuts. If we become fixated on achieving plans or fulfilling our desires, emotions can cause us to make unwise decisions. Acknowledging the time required and being willing to exercise the necessary patience can be the difference between success and failure. Looking again at one of the passages above, we are told, *"The plans of the diligent lead to profit as surely as haste leads to poverty"* (Proverbs 21:5). Yet another translation of the same passage states, *"Good planning and hard work lead to prosperity, but hasty shortcuts lead to poverty."*

Maintain a forward-looking attitude. We can either become caught up in the moment and what we haven't yet achieved, or remain focused on our ultimate goal, just as a marathon runner ignores pain and weariness by concentrating on the finish line ahead. *"Brethren, I do not regard myself as having laid hold of it yet; but one thing I do: forgetting what lies behind and reaching forward to what lies ahead, I press on toward the goal for the prize of the upward call of God in Christ Jesus"* (Philippians 3:13-14).

PUTTING IT INTO PRACTICE

1. "The best things always take time." Do you agree with this state-
    ment? Can you think of any notable exceptions to this principle?
    Is attaining wisdom always a product of time?

2. Think of something you're engaged in that is requiring of you
    a substantial investment of time, energy, and perhaps personal
    resources. Do you think the dividends you'll reap from this in-
    vestment will prove worthwhile? Explain your answer.

3. What other examples come to your mind of things that can't be
    realized through shortcuts or trying to minimize the amount of
    time required for achieving them?

4. How can or should a person deal with periods of discourage-
    ment when hopes and dreams, goals and objectives are proving
    to take longer to become reality than expected? Can you offer an
    example from your own experience?

CHAPTER 46

ROOTED TOGETHER FOR STRENGTH

I 've never had the opportunity to see firsthand the huge sequoia trees, also known as California redwoods, that grow in the western United States. However, I recently learned of a characteristic these trees have that contributes not only to their incredible height but also to their extraordinary longevity.

These trees have been known to grow well over 300 feet tall (not including their root system), up to 26 feet in diameter, and many have lived well beyond 1,000 years. To what do scientists attribute their amazing size, durability and lifespan? One of the most important factors, I discovered, is their root system. Sequoia trees intertwine their roots with other sequoias, enabling them to share strength and resources necessary for their growth and health. They're better equipped for enduring adversity as well.

What if we were to function more like sequoias in the business and professional world? There's a tendency to emphasize independence and celebrate individual achievement. We hear about the "rising star" in the office or company, the person that stands out for exceptional performance. There's nothing wrong with recognizing those that stand out, but a reality in both nature and everyday life is in virtually every instance, we can accomplish more together than we could by operating independently.

Despite mantras such as "it is all about me" and "I did it my way," there's something very gratifying and rewarding about working together as a team, complementing one another with our respective strengths and abilities, and offsetting our weaknesses. Every visionary leader needs good administrative, clerical and support staff to accomplish their objectives. Idea people need skilled communicators to convey their concepts effectively. Accomplished sales people would be of no value without the capable workers poised to make the products they sell.

The Bible emphasizes this principle of pooling resources and mutual strength for a greater outcome. Here is a sampling of what it says about working together for the common good, much as huge sequoias merge root systems to maximize their growth:

Joining together to provide needed support. We need each other. Isolation and insistence on operating alone can ultimately lead to discouragement and lack of motivation. We also get off course more easily. *"And let us consider how we may spur one another on toward love and good deeds. Let us not give up meeting together, as some are in the habit of doing, but let us encourage one another"* (Hebrews 10:24-25).

Sharing resources for mutual benefit. In a competitive world, we're tempted to seek our own advantage, at times at the expense of others. But short-term gains can result in long-term losses. Working together, sharing assets and strengths, can lead to substantially greater benefits for all. *"And do not forget to do good and to share with others, for with such sacrifices God is pleased"* (Hebrews 13:16).

Teaming up to achieve greater results. There is much to be said about the synergy of people working in concert, united around a common sense of mission, vision and values. They can accomplish great things together that they could only dream about independently. *"Two are better than one, because they have a good return for their work. If one falls down, his friend can help him up. But pity the man who falls and has no one to help him up?... Though one may be overpowered, two can defend themselves. A cord of three strands is not quickly broken"* (Ecclesiastes 4:9-12).

PUTTING IT INTO PRACTICE

1. Have you ever personally seen sequoia trees or studied character-istics of their unique growth and longevity? What do you know about them?

2. Can you think of a time or situation in which the principle of being "rooted together" was clearly demonstrated during the course of a project you were involved with at work? Describe the circumstances and the outcome.

3. When might it be better to insist on working independently, rather than as part of a team? Do you think the desire for per-sonal gain and benefits could justify that approach at times? Or are there times when it might be more productive to work alone? Why or why not?

4. How can working with others toward achieving a common mis-sion enhance personal motivation, inspiration and strength? Give any examples that come to your mind.

CHAPTER 47

WHAT ARE YOU WORKING FOR?

People go to work for many different reasons. One primary reason, obviously, is to earn a livelihood – putting food on the table, a roof over their heads, paying bills, and achieving their desired lifestyle. Without question, work also gives us something to do – a way to utilize and invest our time on a regular basis.

Work also can give us a sense of self-worth, the satisfaction of being able to achieve something worthwhile – especially if it involves tasks we are uniquely or specially equipped to perform. If you have work that you enjoy, you're among the fortunate minority of workers; a very happy group. But have you ever gone to work yearning for recognition, even hoping to earn honors or awards that would signify that you were the best – or one of the best – in your company, or even your profession?

When I was editing a magazine, I would attend an annual publisher's conference. One evening session each year included an awards contest where periodicals, writers and editors were judged and recognized in various categories. Occasionally our magazine received an honor, and that was gratifying. But have you ever thought about how fleeting such recognition is – even in the most prestigious competitions?

For instance: Can you name the athletes chosen Most Valuable Player in the last five Super Bowls? Or the teams that captured the last 10 World Cup championships? Can you name the women selected to represent your country in the last five Miss Universe pageants? How about the last five Nobel Prize winners in economics, science, or any other field of endeavor? What were the names of the last five films to receive the Academy Award for motion picture of the year?

We could think of many other examples. We like recognition. It affirms us, making us feel valued and significant. But awards and recognition are soon forgotten. Applause fades, good feelings disappear, and everyone searches for the newest "star." King Solomon, the writer of the Old Testament book of Ecclesiastes, declared, *"for all is vanity and a striving after wind"* (Ecclesiastes 2:17).

Does this mean the pursuit of excellence and personal fulfillment is futile, a complete waste of time and effort? The Bible tells us striving to do our best is important, but our motivations are what matters most:

Performing for an audience of one. People – even our employers and coworkers – are fickle. We can't please them all the time. So we need to make certain we're working for the approval of the right person. *"Whatever you do, work at it with all your heart, as working for the Lord, not for men.... It is the Lord Christ you are serving"* (Colossians 3:23-24).

Receiving God's commendation. In the real world, sometimes our best work is overlooked or ignored. But the Bible assures us God notices all we do for Him and is eager to reward us for devoted service. *"His master replied, 'Well done, good and faithful servant! You have been faithful with a few things; I will put you in charge of many things...'"* (Matthew 25:21,23).

Gaining recognition that endures. The problem with many awards and honors is they lose value and luster over time. History collects dust and tarnishes. God's recognition, however, never fades or diminishes in worth. It is eternal. *"And when the Chief Shepherd appears, you will receive the crown of glory that will never fade away"* (1 Peter 5:4).

PUTTING IT INTO PRACTICE

1. Describe your primary reasons for going to work each day. Have these basic motives and rationales changed during your career?

2. Has the desire to receive recognition been one of your primary motivations for the work you do, whether to be noticed and commended by the person you work for, or to earn prestige within your company or your industry? Explain your answer.

3. Why do you think the "life span" of recognition is so short, that we can be so quick to forget even the most notable accomplishments? How does this affect your own need for recognition and rewards?

4. What's your reaction to the idea of striving first and foremost to serve and please God through our work, being content with receiving His commendation?

CHAPTER 48

THE PERVASIVE POWER OF PERSISTENCE

What would you consider the foremost requirement for success in the workplace? Would it be talent? Or education? Training? Good luck?

Certainly each of these can be a factor in professional success. But there's one other quality that might be more important than all of them – *persistence*. Richard M. DeVos, Sr., co-founder of the Amway Corporation and owner of the National Basketball Association's Orlando Magic, offered this perspective:

"If I had to select one quality, one personal characteristic that I regard as being most highly correlated with success, whatever the field, I would pick the trait of persistence. Determination. The will to endure to the end, to get knocked down 70 times and get up off the floor saying, 'Here comes number 71!'"

DeVos seems to have a good point. If we think of top achievers in virtually any pursuit – government, business, technology, science, medicine, even sports and entertainment – we find most of them did not become "overnight successes," but made their marks through hard work and a resolve never to accept failure as a final verdict. When we read the biographies of famous people, we usually discover they utilized adversity as motivation to keep trying, rather than as an excuse for quitting.

I have a friend who overcame great disadvantages in childhood and young adulthood to forge a very successful career as an entrepreneur and sales executive. Despite a limited education and a lack of training, he embarked on a rigorous self-improvement program, proving wrong scoffers that insisted he was doomed to fail. Persistence, even in the face of setbacks, was his constant companion and greatest asset.

The Bible has much to say about persistence and its close cousin, perseverance. For instance:

Persistence builds character. Just as persistence in exercise strengthens and tones muscles, persistence in the face of everyday challenges and obstacles builds character and inner strength. *"...but we also rejoice in our sufferings, because we know that suffering produces perseverance; perseverance, character; and character, hope. And hope does not disappoint us..."* (Romans 5:3-5).

Persistence provides joy. Staying the course, refusing to give up, and then reaping the fruits of hard work and determination, provide a sense of joy and fulfillment that cannot be achieved in any other way. *"Consider it pure joy, my brothers, whenever you face trials of many kinds, because you know that the testing of your faith develops perseverance. Perseverance must finish its work so that you may be mature and complete, not lacking anything"* (James 1:2-4).

Persistence reinforces purpose. When we focus on specific goals and an overriding, clearly defined mission, they help us to persevere despite bouts with discouragement and disappointment. As DeVos said, we can get knocked down 70 times and get up again. *"Brothers, I do not consider myself yet to have taken hold of it. But one thing I do: Forgetting what is behind and straining toward what is ahead. I press on toward the goal to win the prize for which God has called me heavenward in Christ Jesus"* (Philippians 3:13-14).

Putting It into Practice

1. What do you think of Richard DeVos's statement that persistence is the quality or characteristic he believes correlates most directly to success?

2. Think of a time when persistence played an important role in your quest to reach a certain goal or objective. What difference did it make to execute and maintain that kind of determination?

3. How do you think persistence and perseverance can build character?

4. Do you agree with the statement that persistence can provide a sense of joy that cannot be obtained or experienced in any other way? Why or why not?

CHAPTER 49

WHAT ARE YOUR BEST PRACTICES?

In today's business and professional world, we often hear companies talk about "best practices" that can distinguish them from their competitors. One definition of this term is "a method or technique that has consistently shown results superior to those achieved with other means, and that is used as a benchmark...a 'best' practice can evolve to become better as improvements are discovered."

There is wisdom in any organization resolving to assess its best practices, not only for how it compares with others, but also to determine how it can enhance what it's already doing. Perhaps you're involved some way in doing that where you work. But I wonder if it would make sense for each of us to evaluate our "best practices" as individuals as well.

Years ago I had been working for a non-profit for several years when a one of the top executives I was meeting with asked how I envisioned my future with the organization. The question caught me by surprise, because I was not intending to "climb the corporate ladder." In my role as a writer and editor, I felt fulfilled and confident I was exactly where I was best suited for supporting the organization's goals and objectives.

At that time, my "best practice" was to understand what I was most qualified to do and what work I found most meaningful and rewarding. To strive for a more prestigious role would have meant doing less of what I enjoyed and assuming more administrative responsibilities. While I recognized those as noble and necessary pursuits, I had a clear understanding that wasn't the course I wanted to take. As I've noted earlier, Oswald Chambers, one of my favorite writers, made the declaration many years ago that, "Good is the enemy of the best." A promotion would have been a good thing, but for me it wouldn't have been the *best* thing.

I have found the Bible speaks directly to this idea of "best practices" for us as individuals. Here are several examples:

We come into this life with a special purpose. It is humbling to consider that even before we were born, God had a special plan in mind for our lives. What we do – and what we're good at doing – isn't an accident. *"For you created my inmost being; you knit me together in my mother's womb. I praise you because I am fearfully and wonderfully made"* (Psalm 139:13-14). *"For we are God's workmanship, created in Christ Jesus to do good works, which God prepared in advance for us to do"* (Ephesians 2:10).

We function best while working in concert with others. In any organization, some people have more visible, prestigious roles, but every job can be significant for achieving the corporate mission. *"But in fact God has arranged the parts of the body, every one of them, just as he wanted them to be. If they were all one part, where would the body be? As it is, there are many parts, but one body"* (1 Corinthians 12:18-20).

We work most effectively when using our gifts and abilities to the fullest. When we are using the skills and capabilities that we've discovered are uniquely and innately ours, we can perform our responsibilities with much enthusiasm and passion. In doing so, over time we'll receive recognition for the quality of our work – and will be able to do more of it. *"Do you see a man skilled in his work? He will serve before kings; he will not serve before obscure men"* (Proverbs 22:29).

PUTTING IT INTO PRACTICE

1. When you hear the term "best practices," what comes to your mind?

2. Do you agree with idea that "best practices" can be applied to individuals, as well as companies and organizations? Why or why not?

3. We've revisited Oswald Chambers' statement, "Good is the enemy of the best." How might that apply to your life, either professionally or personally? How difficult is it to discern what the "best" things are for you – and do you often find it challenging to maintain your focus on them, when "good" opportunities are presented?

4. How do you respond to the assertion that we each have a special, divinely ordained plan and purpose for our lives?

CHAPTER 50

NO GOLD TO BE GLEANED FROM GOSSIP

When managers and supervisors are surveyed about the most pervasive problems they must address in the workplace, one that typically ranks near the top of the list is gossip. One definition for *gossip* is "idle talk or rumor, especially about the personal or private affairs of others." So the objective of gossip in the workplace is definitely not team-building.

The content of such gossip can range from job performance to workplace attire to "office politics" to speculating on behind-the-scenes relationships between colleagues. In many cases, none of these discussions contribute to higher levels of productivity or camaraderie. But that does not reduce the temptation to share juicy secrets about other staff not present to hear what is being said about them.

"You will never guess what I just heard about…!" "Did you know that … and her husband are having problems?" "I was talking to Jim yesterday, and he told me that … is on the verge of being terminated." "Have you noticed Marvin has been acting strangely lately? Do you think he might be drinking again?" Can you recall any "information sharing" examples like these you have heard recently? How do you feel when you hear them?

People often talk about being overloaded with work, but somehow they still find time to talk behind their coworkers' backs. Perhaps speaking disparagingly about others helps to enhance their own self-esteem.

Or it might be the attraction of possessing "inside information" others do not have; if you fail to share it, how will they know you have it, right? Rarely, if ever, does gossip have positive value. It diminishes the object of the conversation, and the end result may also diminish the reputation of the one offering negative comments. Here are some insights about gossip and the wayward tongue, along with warnings presented in the Bible:

Gossip reflects a lack of good judgment. Just because we know – or suspect – something about another person, that doesn't mean we have an obligation to express our suspicions to others. *"The tongue of the righteous is choice silver, but the heart of the wicked is of little value. The lips of the righteous nourish many, but fools die for lack of judgment"* (Proverbs 10:20-21).

Gossip destroys trust. Sometimes a colleague will share information in private, trusting that knowledge will be kept in secret. A decision to be indiscreet and pass that information along to others can forever destroy a professional or personal relationship. *"A man who lacks judgment derides his neighbor, but a man of understanding holds his tongue. A gossip betrays a confidence, but a trustworthy man keeps a secret"* (Proverbs 11:12-13). *"A perverse man stirs up dissension, and a gossip separates close friends"* (Proverbs 16:28).

Gossip can sometimes wound more deeply than a physical weapon. As noted previously, the old saying, "Sticks and stones may break my bones, but words will never hurt me," is untrue. Often the damage resulting from harsh, uncaring, or even thoughtless comments can result is considerable emotional, relational and even spiritual injury. *"Reckless words pierce like a sword, but the tongue of the wise brings healing"* (Proverbs 12:18).

Gossip, even if unintended, can bring consequences greater than ever imagined. Even if our motives are not to cause harm to someone, recklessly expressed words can prove to be surprisingly destructive. *"Consider what a great forest is set on fire by a small spark. The tongue also is a fire, a world of evil among the parts of the body. It corrupts the whole person, sets the whole course of his life on fire, and is itself set on fire by hell"* (James 3:5-6). *"He who guards his lips guards his life, but he who speaks rashly will come to ruin"* (Proverbs 13:3).

PUTTING IT INTO PRACTICE

1. Have you found gossip to be a problem where you work, either at present or in the past? If so, explain some of the difficulties or conflicts that can result from gossip.

2. Why do you think that having to deal with gossip is such a common challenge in workplace settings?

3. If you find yourself in a meeting with fellow workers and the topic of discussion turns into gossip, how do you typically react? Do you find yourself participating in it, do you just quietly listen, or do you take some form of action to discourage the person or persons involved in gossiping? Explain your answer.

4. What guidelines that you have adopted personally or taken from the Bible could be used in attempting to stop an exchange or escalation of gossip? Do you think it is even your responsibility to discourage people from gossiping about other people? Why or why not?

CHAPTER 51

DO YOU DESIRE TO GO FAST – OR GO FAR?

Not long ago I had an opportunity to view an excellent film, "The Good Lie," based on the true story of a small group of Sudanese refugees who had fled tyranny in their homeland and ultimately found a new home for themselves in Kansas City, Missouri. At the conclusion of the movie, an African proverb was displayed that summarized their amazing pilgrimage:

"If you want to go fast, go alone. If you want to go far, go together."

Sixteen simple words, but they are infused with wisdom and truth. When I read them, my first thought was of Olympic competitions. In sprinting events, runners compete individually with the sole objective of arriving at the finish line first. However, in relay races, as well as longer endurance events like marathons, participants run in groups, whether as teams or to provide mutual support for the arduous competition. To succeed over the long haul, it seems much better to go together than to go alone.

When I was a magazine editor, I usually wrote articles alone. However, when the time came to design the magazine and get it ready for publication, we had a talented team that merged our creative talents. When we were finished, the result was amazing: The whole was always greater than the sum of the parts.

In the business and professional world we often hear stories about visionary entrepreneurs who set ambitious goals. For a time they may do well, going fast while being independent. However, to fully realize their dreams, even innovative entrepreneurs need people that can bring their dreams to reality, whether it involves computer technology, developing new ways for manufacturing products, or designing a clothing line.

Years ago vocalist Frank Sinatra recorded a hit song with the refrain, "I Did It My Way." However, even the late Mr. Sinatra needed many people – musicians, composers, backup singers, administrative staff, publicists and others to sustain his career of more than 60 years.

In business circles we often hear about climbing the "ladder of success." There are two curious things about this "ladder of success," however. In the process of climbing, as some have noted, we'll find ourselves crossing paths with others that have already gone as high as they can and are on the way back down. Also, if the ladder is very high, you need someone else to hold it steady so you don't fall off. You can't climb the ladder alone.

The Bible offers many examples of people who had the wisdom to go far together – Moses and Joshua, Elijah and Elisha, Jesus and His disciples, Barnabas and Paul, Paul and Timothy. We also find examples of men who tried to go fast alone and failed miserably in the latter stages of their lives – King David and his son, King Solomon, are among the most notable. Here are some pertinent principles from the Bible:

We can bring out the best in each other. In collaborating to achieve a common goal, we help one another to become more productive and effective; even creative conflict and friction can prove to be valuable. *"As iron sharpens iron, so one man sharpens another"* (Proverbs 27:17).

We can accomplish more together. Just as a flock of geese is able to travel long distances with each individual goose taking a turn in doing the work of leading, a team of people in business can accomplish much more over long periods of time by joining together in a united, concerted effort. *"Two are better than one, because they have a good return for their work.... A cord of three strands is not quickly broken"* (Ecclesiastes 4:9-12).

PUTTING IT INTO PRACTICE

1. Before reading this chapter, were you familiar with the African proverb, "If you want to go fast, go alone. If you want to go far, go together"? What specifically does it say to you?

2. Can you think of an example – perhaps from your own experience – of someone who seemed to be going fast alone, but because he or she wasn't working in concert with other people, ultimately failed to realize the long-term success they had anticipated? If so, describe that situation.

3. What are some benefits of being able to say, as the song declares, "I did it my way"? What are some of the disadvantages?

4. The proverb from the Bible states, "As iron sharpens iron, one man (or woman) sharpens another." What does that really mean in a practical sense, from your perspective? Have you experienced something like that in your own career, someone sharpening you as you worked together?

CHAPTER 52

BE CAREFUL HOW YOU LEAD...
OR HOW YOU FOLLOW

Recently I read a brief account about a sheep in Istanbul, Turkey that jumped off a cliff. What made the story especially tragic was nearly 1,500 other sheep followed, about one-third of them dying as a result. Most of the remaining sheep suffered injuries. Afterward all of the survivors must have been wondering sheepishly, "What was I thinking?"

In case you surmise this must have been an aberration, a rarity in the world of sheep, be assured it was not. My friend, Ken Johnson, wrote a book called *Pursuing Life With a Shepherd's Heart,* and recounted many examples of how foolish sheep are. He recounted one experience that relates directly to the sheep-over-the-cliff incident.

Early one morning Ken was preparing to let his sheep out of their barn. As the first sheep came to the doorway, he held the handle of a hoe in front of it to see what it would do. The sheep casually jumped over the hoe handle and proceeded to amble toward the pasture. Ken then pulled the handle away, but as each sheep exited the barn, it paused at the same spot and then jumped, just as the sheep in front of it had done, and then walked forward. Apparently sheep follow the leader's example, regardless of whether it makes sense to do so.

What does this have to do with today's workplace? A lot. We have a common tendency to play "follow the leader" regardless of whether there's good reason for it. We adopt the latest business philosophies because everyone else is doing it. We use the newest technological device, often simply because someone else has decided to use it. When we enter a store, we unthinkingly get in line – because everyone else is in line.

Apparently our behavior strongly resembles the wooly creatures we call sheep. The Bible even asserts, *"We all, like sheep, have gone astray…"* (Isaiah 41:10). The Scriptures present numerous comparisons between sheep and people, pointing out sheep are desperately dependent on a shepherd.

What this tells us is to be cautious about whom we follow, so we're not led astray – and if we're in leadership roles, to take seriously and soberly our responsibility to properly "shepherd" those entrusted to our care and direction. Here are a few principles the Bible offers:

We all need a shepherd. We tend to believe we can function perfectly well on our own, without the assistance or guidance of anyone. But like sheep, we all can become misguided by wrong thinking, motives and objectives. *"When he saw the crowds, he (Jesus) had compassion on them, because they were harassed and helpless, like sheep without a shepherd'* (Matthew 9:36).

Be careful which shepherds you follow. Some people in positions of leadership can sound very convincing, assuring us they have our best interests at heart. We must be cautious, however, to make certain we really want to go where they're wanting to lead us. *"My people have been lost sheep, their shepherds have led them astray and caused them to roam…and (they) forgot their resting place"* (Jeremiah 50:6).

The right shepherd is one we can trust. The shepherd worth following remains with us, joining and leading us through times of challenge and adversity. He won't abandon us when times become difficult. Jesus was the ultimate example: *"I am the good shepherd. The good shepherd lays down his life for the sheep. The hired hand is not the shepherd who owns the sheep. So when he sees the wolf coming, he abandons the sheep and runs away…. I know my sheep and my sheep know me – just as the Father knows me and I know the Father – and I lay down my life for the sheep"* (John 10:11-14).

Putting It into Practice

1. Have you ever found yourself doing something, even adopting a business practice, simply because everyone else was doing it, then later questioning the wisdom of doing so? If so, what was the situation – and what was the outcome?

2. Can you think of a time, whether in your personal experience or just a circumstance you witnessed or heard about, when – like the sheep following the single sheep that jumped off the cliff – people were enticed by a poor leader with disastrous results?

3. Do you consider yourself a "shepherd" to others, whether at work or in your home? How well do you think you're carrying out that responsibility? Explain your answer.

4. Jesus Christ described Himself as the Good Shepherd. What is your reaction to that claim – and what do you think He meant in saying that?

CHAPTER 53

IMPOSSIBLE IS NOT POSSIBLE – UNTIL YOU QUIT

How many times have you heard someone in the workplace make this declaration: "We can't do that. It is not possible"? Sometimes this is true – a customer makes a demand that can't possibly be satisfied within the specified time frame. Or a client asks for a service far beyond your company's expertise. Often, however, we conclude something isn't possible because it seems like too much work, we don't know whether it can be done, or fear putting forth the effort only to fail.

My friend, Gary Highfield, has written an outstanding book called *When 'Want To' Becomes 'Have To!'*, his story of overcoming formidable odds to become a successful business leader: He never knew his biological father and had a very unsettled childhood, even witnessing devastating family tragedy while he was a boy. Despite these hardships, and motivated by financial adversity he encountered as a young husband and father, Gary undertook a methodical, very determined strategy for dramatically changing his circumstances.

He discovered many useful life principles during this process, including this declaration: "Impossible is not possible – until you quit." This seven-word statement seems simple, but it's profound. Time and again, people told Gary what he wouldn't be able to do, such as becoming a top-producing, industry-leading salesman, an entrepreneur, small business owner, and even a commercial loan officer. Yet he succeeded in achieving each of these goals. All because he refused to believe that what he wanted to do was impossible.

There are many other examples of people who ignored negative voices, who recognized that what people said was "impossible" was in fact possible – unless they quit trying. Michelangelo probably had his detractors when he embarked on painting the ceiling of the Sistine Chapel. Thomas Edison made multiple attempts at inventing an incandescent light bulb until he succeeded. He refused to stop trying.

In 1943, IBM chairman Thomas Watson stated, "I think there is a world market for maybe five computers." And Digital Equipment Corp. founder Ken Olson said in 1977, "There is no reason anyone would want a computer in their home." However, through hard work, vision and innovation – understanding *impossible is not possible until you quit* – many men and women proved these well-known, one-time industry giants wrong. In fact, the way this book was published became possible because they were wrong about what was "impossible."

The Bible directly addresses this issue. Faith in and dependence on God, it declares, can move the "impossible" into reality:

We cannot do it through our own resources alone. The fact is that many of our desired goals often are unattainable in our own strength. They aren't impossible, but require more than the power we can muster within ourselves. We need power beyond ourselves. *"I can do everything through (Christ) who strengthens me"* (Philippians 4:13).

We can – but only with God. If you have a God-sized dream or goal, accomplishing it requires willingness to turn to the God who gave you the dream. As Jesus told His followers, *"With man this is impossible, but not with God; all things are possible with God"* (Mark 10:27).

We need the right motivation. It makes sense sometimes to ask ourselves, "Why am I doing this? Why is accomplishing this so important to me?" If our inspiration is not self-gratification, but rather our desire to serve, please and honor God, we can rely on and trust in His divine assistance and direction. *"Delight yourself in the Lord and He will give you the desires of your heart"* (Psalm 37:4).

PUTTING IT INTO PRACTICE

1. Do you know someone, perhaps yourself, who has overcome considerable personal and professional adversity and setbacks to achieve great success? How have they – or you – accomplished that?

2. What is your reaction to the statement, "Impossible is not possible – until you quit"?

3. Think of some other examples of people's achievements that at one time were considered impossible, even unthinkable. What do you think motivated these people to achieve their dreams and objectives, despite formidable obstacles and opposition from others?

4. It is suggested that seemingly impossible things can be accomplished through God's power and guidance. Do you agree? Do you think God even cares about our goals and challenges? Why or why not?

Afterword

I sn't it amazing how a small book – even one little portion of the Bible like Proverbs – has such relevance and meaning for today's business and professional world? There's only one explanation, in my mind: God's truth is timeless. Despite the continuous passage of years and centuries, His eternal principles for life and work remain unaffected by the shifting tides of business trends, innovative strategies, and technological breakthroughs.

Iron Age. Industrial Age. Information Age. No matter. The realities of human nature remain constant, as do the foundational truths and principles the Creator put in place for guiding and governing His creation.

My hope is that through these 53 chapters you have gained a new or renewed appreciation for the significance and importance of the Scriptures for the 21st century marketplace, and for life in general.

These pages, however, have barely tapped the depth of wisdom we find in the book of Proverbs, or the other 65 books in the Bible. Perhaps this has whetted your appetite for learning more about what God has presented to us in His Word about the world of work.

In the Old Testament we see in Joseph a wonderful example of commitment, loyalty, moral purity, vision, and long-range planning. Moses and Joshua model the art of delegation and crisis management. Nehemiah offers strong lessons in how to prepare for a major project, assess underlying necessities and issues, and how to assemble and lead a team to successfully achieve the goal despite eager detractors. King David shows the importance of honestly facing up to major failures, how to cope with strong opposition, and the role of faith in decision-making. In Ecclesiastes, King Solomon, who wrote much of Proverbs, emphasizes teamwork and the need for a balanced, proper perspective on work and other areas of life. Daniel demonstrates the virtues of integrity and dedication to a mission.

In the New Testament, Jesus taught and served as the ultimate example of servant leadership and self-sacrifice, along with imparting invaluable principles about team building, leadership development, followership, financial and fiscal management, strategic planning, and goal-setting. No one has ever approached Jesus in His skill for formulating a clearly understood, compelling vision and mission. These principles were further expounded in letters written by many of His followers, including Paul, James, Peter and John.

I'm convinced that the unfathomable depth of the Bible makes it the greatest book of all – not only for business and the workplace, but also for every other aspect of life.

There are those, I know, who would still argue that the Word of God isn't relevant or practical for contemporary living. My response would be simply that they obviously have not read the Scriptures or honestly considered what they have to say to us in the 21st century – or any century, for that matter. As with peeling an onion, removing one layer only to find multiple layers underneath, the Scriptures also can be read and understood one layer of truth after another, never to be exhausted during the course of an entire lifetime.

Over the past 30 years or so, the publishing world has exploded with hundreds of books that address the intersection of work and spirituality, the merging of vocation and faith. Many are filled with valuable insights for the office, the retail center, and the boardroom. But I would highly recommend that you consult the original source, the Bible, to see what God Himself has to say.

As King David wrote in one of his Psalms:

"Your word, O Lord, is eternal, it stands firm in the heavens…. Your laws endure to this day, for all things serve you…. Your word is a lamp

to my feet and a light for my path.... The unfolding of your words gives light, it gives understanding to the simple.... Your words are true; all your righteous laws are eternal..." (Psalm 119:89,91,105,160).

ABOUT THE AUTHOR

Robert J. Tamasy has enjoyed a multi-faceted career as a veteran journalist for more than 40 years. After graduating from the Ohio State University with two degrees in journalism, he spent 10 years as an editor for community newspapers in suburbs of Columbus, Ohio, Houston, Texas, and Philadelphia, Pa.

He served 17 years as publications director for CBMC of USA, also writing and editing *Contact Quarterly* magazine. Then, during Bob's three years as vice president of communications for CBMC International, he began editing and writing "Monday Manna," a weekly workplace meditation that today reaches more than one million business and professional people throughout the world, being translated into more than 20 languages.

Currently vice president of communications for Leaders Legacy, Inc., a non-profit based in Atlanta, Ga. that is dedicated to developing business and professional leaders through mentoring and executive coaching, Bob has written, co-authored and edited more than 20 books. These include *The Heart of Mentoring* (written with David A. Stoddard), *Pursuing Life With a Shepherd's Heart* (with Ken Johnson), *Tufting Legacies* (the story of the Card-Monroe Corp.), *The Complete Christian Businessman, Jesus Works Here,* and *The Powder King* (the story of Pharma Tech Industries).

Bob continues to write and edit "Monday Manna," the original source of the chapters included in *Business At Its Best*. He also has written hundreds of freelance magazine articles, and writes a twice-weekly blog called "Just Thinking."

He and his wife, Sally, live in Chattanooga, Tenn. and have five children, 10 grandchildren and one great-grandchild.

Bob can be contacted at btamasy@gmail.com.
He writes two blogs. Their addresses are:
www.bobtamasy.blogspot.com
www.bobtamasy.wordpress.com

To subscribe to the "Monday Manna" meditations and receive them each week by email, visit the www.cbmcint.org website.